PUNchline

How to Think Like a Humorist If You're Humor Impaired

Paul E. McGhee, Ph.D.

KENDALL/HUNT PUBLISHING COMPANY
2460 Kerper Boulevard P.O. Box 539 Dubuque, Iowa 52004-0539

Clipart images from CorelDraw 3.0 were used in the preparation of this book.

Copyright © 1993 by Paul E. McGhee

Library of Congress Catalog Card Number: 93-77420

ISBN 0-8403-8482-3

All rights reserved. No part of this publication may be reproduced, stored in a retrieval system, or transmitted in any form or by any means, electronic, mechanical, photocopying, recording, or otherwise, without the prior written permission of the copyright owner.

Printed in the United States of America
10   9   8   7   6   5   4   3   2   1

"A sharp tongue is the only edged tool that grows keener with constant use."

Washington Irving

CONTENTS

Introduction i

1. Children's Riddles and Jokes 1

2. Mixed Children's Riddles and Jokes 15

3. Puns 23

4. Jokes 33

5. Stories and Longer Jokes 65

INTRODUCTION

> *"The most completely lost of all days is the one on which we have not laughed."*
>
> French proverb

Are you humor impaired? Do you find it impossible to remember a joke or funny story? Have you been known to go an entire decade without a witty remark? Are you always the last one to get jokes told by others? When other people describe you, do they say that you have "terminal seriousness?" Do you often find yourself wondering what everyone else is laughing at? Have you ever been at the movies, and found yourself thinking, "Wait a minute, is this satire?" If you answered "yes" to any of these questions, then you may be humor impaired. This book is designed to help you leave the ranks of the humor impaired by enabling you to start thinking like a humorist. By giving you over 350 opportunities to stretch your humor skills, this book provides you the practical experience of thinking the same way a joke writer thinks when writing new material.

We all love to be around people who make us laugh. At parties and other social occasions, those who are gifted in telling jokes and stories, or creating spontaneous witticisms, invariably have a crowd around them. At some point in your life, you've probably found yourself thinking, "Boy, I wish I could do that." If you're like most people, you think you're either born with a good sense of humor, or you're not. And if you're not, you're automatically relegated to the camp of those who enjoy the jokes, stories, and spontaneous wit of others. What you don't realize is that witty people and great joke tellers have been working at it most of their life. They've had a lot of practice! You, on the other hand, have never made any effort to improve your ability to remember jokes and stories, or create your own spontaneous humor.

How This Book Will Improve Your Ability to Create Humor

Have you ever wondered why all the jokes you've heard and read over the years never nurtured your own ability to create humor? The reason is that just hearing or reading a joke gives you no opportunity to extend your own creative thinking skills. It gives you no chance to exercise your own ability to come up with something that would make it funny.

We are generally presented with the entire joke on a silver platter. Even as kids, we rarely came up with our own riddles (the ones we did create weren't funny). We just faithfully told the ones we heard from others. If you've had children of your own, you know that many of the same jokes you heard as a kid are still circulating today.

This book will help improve your ability to create original humor spontaneously by giving you repeated opportunities to do what humorists and comedy writers do — come up with your own funny lines. The most important feature of the book is that it does most — but not all — of the work for you by setting up a context in which everything is provided except a key word or phrase which completes the PUNchline. You provide the PUNchline. A clue is provided to help you focus your thoughts in the right direction. Once you've made the effort to come up with your own answer, you can check the answer given in the back of that section.

The reason this approach works is that it calls attention to the different types of thinking that are involved in the creation off a joke. In the seminars and workshops I provide on humor and stress to hospitals and corporations around the country, a common complaint is that "I just can't think of a funny line. No matter how hard I try, I just can't think that way." By the time you get to the age you are now, you've had years of practice at thinking in a "straight" direction. To do humor, you've got to learn to think "crooked." You have to learn to play with words and ideas. You need experience at exaggeration, understatement, reversal, and other traditional techniques of making up jokes.

When we were children, we all loved to play. We could spend all day playing. Most of this play was physical, but as we got older we learned that playing with ideas was fun too. We all went through the "riddle stage," during which we drove our parents crazy with endless riddles. We found great pleasure in turning the world upside down by distorting things, exaggerating, saying the opposite of what we really meant, and so forth. In order for you to become skilled at creating your own verbal humor now, you need to rediscover that child-like enjoyment of playing with ideas. This book will help you achieve this by getting you actively involved in the actual process of creating humor. As you go through the book, you will find yourself thinking more and more the way a comedy writer or joke writer thinks.

You will know that your ability to "think funny" is growing when you gradually get better at coming up with your own funny answers. These may or may not match the answers provided. But you should not consider your answer wrong if it differs from the one given here. Many jokes and stories can be completed in more than one way and still be funny. And remember, there are no right or wrong answers when it comes to what is funny. If it's funny to you or someone else, then it's funny! Don't worry about it if your sense of humor fails to match someone else's.

You should fight the temptation to simply look up the missing part of the PUNchline without making an effort to think of a funny line yourself. You could go through the entire book this way and have a lot of fun, but you won't improve your humor skills. You'll be no better at creating your own humor after finishing the book than you were before you started it. Improvement will come only if you struggle a bit with each example. As you gain more experience with the kinds of humor represented throughout the book, you will gradually find funny answers popping into your mind with less and less effort. Again, the book is designed to teach you to automatically think like a humorist or comedy writer by channeling your mental associations along lines that are similar to the way humorists think.

How Do Humorists Think?

How do people (like Steve Allen) who are good at coming up with original verbal humor think? They think the way we all thought when we were kids. Humorists love to play with ideas. They like to distort things, or twist them around. They're very flexible mentally, and are much more willing than the rest of us to consider crazy ideas "just to see what happens." They're good at spotting life's absurdities, ironies, and incongruities. They see the ridiculous side of everyday situations that the rest of us take for granted, or don't notice at all.

I argued in my 1979 book <u>Humor: Its Origin and Development</u> (now out of print) that humor is basically play with ideas. A humorist is just a big kid who never stopped playing. S/he just switched from playing physically to playing mentally. And when it comes to playing with ideas, there's no limit! The entire world of our everyday experience is a potential playground.

Humorists especially love to play with language. Language, after all, is our main vehicle for thinking about the world. And while language is not essential to humor, it plays a key role in most humor. Think back to the time (around first grade) that you first realized that words can have more than one meaning. Do you remember how exciting it was to trick someone else in telling riddles? If you come from my generation, you'll recall such groaners as "Why did the moron bury his car?" "Because the engine died." Or, still worse: "Why did the moron jump off the Empire State Building?" "Because he wanted to try out his new spring suit."

This kind of humor, of course, is known as a pun. The reason we groan at puns as adults is precisely because they're generally very simple. Basically, puns are children's humor. And yet this is the level at which you probably stopped developing your own humor skills. Many of us couldn't come up with a spontaneous pun or other funny remark in the next 10 minutes of conversation if our life depended on it. Jack Benny, however, had the following response when a mugger came up to him and shouted, "OK, buddy, your money or your life:" he hesitated, and hesitated, and finally the mugger repeated, "I said, your money or your life." Benny responded, "I'm thinking it over." (Jack Benny was known to be very "tight" with his money.)

This book develops your ability to create verbal humor by starting with puns and other simple joking techniques, first in children's riddles and jokes, and then in adult jokes and stories. With practice, your ability to quickly see potential puns and in everyday language will grow, and this will help you move on to creating other kinds of humor. The rest of the book gives you exposure to the full range of types of humor typically found in adult jokes and stories.

The Nature of Puns

A pun is a play on words that have the same (or similar) sound, but different meanings. The essential ingredient in all puns is ambiguity of the meaning. Many words have more than one meaning, but the context makes the appropriate meaning clear. In riddles and jokes based on puns, we may be led to adopt a meaning that makes no sense, or is absurd, in the context set up by the joke. In some cases, the word is spelled the same way in both meanings. Consider the following joke:

A woman calls up a doctor and says, "Doctor! Doctor! I just swallowed a spoon, what should I do?"

The doctor says, "Sit down and don't stir!"

The key word, obviously, is "stir." We "get" the joke and see the humor in it when we identify the second meaning. The phrase "Sit down and don't stir" normally means to not move around. In this case, though, given that she's swallowed a spoon, the second meaning is technically possible. But the silliness or absurdity of the idea of using a spoon in the stomach to stir like you would stir something in a bowl makes it funny.

In other cases, puns can be based on very different types of ambiguity. For example, we could build jokes around words that are spelled differently, but sound the same (pear/pare/pair). Cunning linguists point out many other ways in which we play with the sound and meaning of words. We will not discuss these here, but the reader will note many different types of puns throughout this book. Knowing the "academic" distinctions made between different puns (e.g., homographic, homophonic) is not essential to learning to develop this part of your sense of humor. A linguistic analysis of word play at the level of phonology, morphology, semantics, syntactics, and pragmatics is not needed to learn how to think of funny lines. The key to becoming a skilled punster or spontaneous wit is best summed up by the well-known story of the teenager who asked someone on the streets of New York how to get to Carnegie Hall. The stranger replied, "Practice, practice, practice." This book gives you that practice.

Learn to Look for Ambiguity

To benefit the most from this book, you should use it not only as a means of exercising your ability to create humor, but as a reminder to be on the lookout for verbal ambiguity in everyday life. The most important lesson to be learned at the start is that everyday language is full of ambiguity. We aren't aware of it as a rule, because the context makes the meaning clear. But that doesn't mean other meanings aren't possible. You want to establish the habit of becoming aware of ambiguity, regardless of whether or not it's funny. This is an important preliminary step to learning to create your own humor based on ambiguity.

The most effective way to establish the habit of detecting ambiguity is to put it on the "front burner" for a few weeks. Carry a notebook around with you and be on the look out for double meanings and ambiguous words or phrases everywhere you go. This will take a conscious effort at first, but you'll soon find yourself noticing them automatically, with no effort at all.

As a preliminary test, consider the sentences below. These are not jokes, but they all contain ambiguity. Determine for yourself how quickly you see the ambiguity. Sentences like this are written and spoken every day. Actively listen and look for them over a period of several weeks. When you get to the point that you perceive them easily and automatically, you will have taken a major step toward strengthening your verbal sense of humor.

- He went deer hunting with a club.
- He helped the woman with the hat.
- The men all laughed at work.
- The restaurant stops serving crabs after 9:30.
- The fat politician's wife loves chocolate.
- The shooting of the Indians was terrible.
  (Find at least three meanings here.)
- The turkey is ready to eat.
- The mayor asked the police stop drinking while driving.

If you make a habit of looking for this kind of ambiguity in conversations and newspapers, even when no one is trying to be funny, you'll find that it will strengthen your ability to guess the PUNchlines in this book. It will also quickly accelerate your ability to come up with your own puns.

Newspapers now commonly play with words in headlines. Here are a few examples:

- "Grandmother of 14 shoots hole in one."
- "Searchers find Big Ugly child."
  (From Big Ugly, W. Va. paper.)
- "Ban on nude dancing on Governor's desk."
- "Furniture drive for homeless launched."

You will also find word play in ads. One ad said: "Braille dictionary for sale. Must see to appreciate."

Even businesses are getting into the act (sometimes unintentionally).

- "Six muffins for $1.50. Limit three per customer."
- "Ask about our layaway plan." (In front of funeral parlor.)
- "Ears pierced while you wait."
- "Use stairs for rest room."
- "Please wash hands before resuming work."
 (In rest room of a state unemployment agency — which also has a cafeteria.)
- "Twenty-five years at same spot."
 (In front of a dry cleaning establishment.)
- "Husband exterminators and pest control."
 (The business is owned by a family named "Husband.")

An excellent exercise you can do whenever you have a spare moment (when you're stuck in traffic, waiting in grocery lines, sitting through a dull meeting or talk, etc.) is to take any word that comes to mind and think of as many meanings as you can come up with for that word. Do this with a partner whenever possible, since your partner will think of meanings you don't think of, and this will further trigger associations of your own in unexpected directions. Whenever possible, write them down as you think of them. The more you do this, the more rapidly you will acquire the habit of thinking of extra unintended meanings of words without really trying.

These strategies are discussed in detail in my upcoming book with Kendall-Hunt (available in late 1993), *How to Develop Your Sense of Humor: An 8-Step program for Learning to Use Humor to Cope with Stress*. This book provides a ready-made program for gradually improving your sense of humor so that you can use it to cope with the common stresses of everyday life. One step of this program focuses on the development of verbal humor skills, but the program itself is designed to improve your ability to find humor in everyday life, to laugh at yourself, and use or find humor in the midst of stress.

Types of Verbal Humor

All humor experts have their own way of classifying "types" of humor. The problem is that any given joke can be classified in several different ways. The following jokes are examples of just a few commonly used classifications.

1) Jokes Based on Word Combinations

A drug company has come up with a new drug. It's half decongestant Anahist, and half tranquilizer Methodone. They're calling it "Methodist."

2) Cross Jokes

What do you get when you cross a turkey with a centipede?
Drumsticks for everybody.

What do you get when you cross a birth control pill with LSD?
A trip without the kids.

3) Daffynitions

What do you call a knife that cuts four loaves of bread at the same time?
A four loaf cleaver.

Defeat: De parts of de body dat are connected to de legs.

4) Differences

What's the difference between the USA and Russia, Poland, Romania, and Czechoslovakia?
The USA has a Communist Party.

5) Exaggeration

Our plane waited on the runway so long they allowed conjugal visits.

"The rain here in Los Angeles has caused a lot of mud slides. I was on my way to work the other day, glanced out the window, and my house was making better time than I was."

6) Light Bulb

How many _____ (fill in your favorite target or victim) does it take to change a light bulb?
Four, one to hold the bulb, and three to turn the ladder.

7) Nonsense

A five-year-old asks his mother if he can watch the solar eclipse. "OK," she says, "But don't stand too close."

8) Reversals

He's so rich that when he writes a check, the bank bounces.

9) Substitution of a Similar Sounding Word

"I was such a great lover on my honeymoon that my wife gave me a standing ovulation."

Other types of classifications could have been included in these examples, but the choice has been made to allow the reader to simply learn by repeated example. Rather than asking you to think about what kind of technique must be used for a joke, the book allows you to focus on finding a funny answer — regardless of the nature of the technique. As you go through example after example, you will begin to find funny PUNchlines occurring to you without ever giving a thought to the kind of technique that would work best. This may be the kind of practice that will serve you best in your everyday life. You want to get to the point that puns and other forms of play with language just pop into mind without any effort on your part. However, some readers will find that they make more rapid progress in improving their own joking skills by asking, "OK, what's going on here? Why is this funny?" In doing this, you will generate your own categories as you go. If you are someone who finds that this makes work out of something that should be fun, then you should by all means avoid any effort to actively question why it's funny, or to generate your own categories.

The list of categories provided here does show that many classification systems are possible. And the same joke can often be classified in many different ways. Many of the jokes and stories included in this book could be fit into two or more of these categories. I initially planned to have separate sections of the book which included only examples of a particular type of humor. It became obvious, however, that this not only makes the jokes and stories repetitive and less fun, it also prevents you from having the opportunity to make your own judgment of what kind of PUNchline is called for in each case. Your own humor skills will develop more rapidly by working with the different techniques in a relatively random order.

Organization of the Book

The initial collection of children's riddles and jokes is designed to give you some experience at guessing the answers to relatively easy riddles and jokes. But even children's riddles are not easy to guess without clues. So don't assume that you're among the humor impaired if you can't guess the answers to these without the help of the clues.

The first group of children's jokes is organized into "categories" in order to give you a clear sense of specific ways of generating verbal humor. The second set of children's jokes is randomly arranged, so that you must come up with a funny PUNchline without having a clue as to the "type" of humor it is. This will help you automatically fall into the mode of humor that best fits the situation set up in the beginning of the joke or story. Most of the jokes and stories in the book are presented in this random fashion. By the time you finish the book, however, you will have been exposed to a broad range of joking techniques.

The third section is entirely composed of puns, in order to assure that you have ample practice at learning to generate puns. A broad range of difficulty is provided here, so you can expect some successes and some failures. A few children's jokes or riddles have also been included here.

The fourth section consists of jokes and brief stories typical of adult humor. A range of techniques is again provided here, including some puns. The final section consists of stories and longer jokes. These stories also include a broad range of humor techniques.

How to Use This Book

To benefit the most from this book, you must resist the temptation to simply look up the PUNchline at the end of that section. Cover up the clue which follows the joke, and give yourself 30 seconds to come up with some kind of joking answer. Then check the clue. If you come up with an answer without looking at the clue, the clue will either confirm what you were thinking, or point you in some new direction. If you fail to come up with an answer, the mental effort you've made will still help you improve your humor skills (especially if you do this throughout the book). After reading the clue, give yourself another 30 seconds to come up with an answer before checking the one given in the book.

Remember, you may come up with PUNchlines that are just as funny (or funnier!) than the ones provided here. Many jokes have more than one possible funny ending, so don't fall into thinking that there's a "right" or "wrong" answer. Also, keep in mind that the readers who will benefit the most from going through this book are the ones who make the effort to think of a funny answer on their own. If you treat this like any other joke book, you'll have some laughs, but you won't develop your own ability to create humor.

You will discover that trying to think of funny PUNchlines is mentally tiring at first. So do not try to read the book at one sitting. Put it in a place where you can spend 15-30 minutes with it before going on to something else. Otherwise, you'll fall into the habit of just looking up the answer without trying to think of one yourself. Make the mental effort to come up with answers on your own. The more you do so, the more easily and automatically puns and other kinds of humor will come to you.

Also, if you adopt the habit of looking up the answer without trying to think of one yourself, you rob yourself of your only opportunity to really gain from the book. Once you have seen the answer given here, it is no longer possible to "stretch" your own humor skills. As you read the jokes the second time, you'll automatically be drawn toward trying to remember the answer you saw the first time you read the joke.

Once you have finished the book, let it sit for a month or more, and then come back to it and go through all the examples again. You will remember many of the answers, but going through the motions of generating the answer again — even from memory — will help consolidate the gains toward thinking like a humorist that you made the first time through the book.

CHILDREN'S RIDDLES AND JOKES

Puns

1) What time is it when an elephant sits on your fence?
   Clue: "Time" here does not refer to time of day.

2) What is it that is bought by the yard, but worn by the foot?
   Clue: The word "foot" does not refer to 12 inches.
   Extra Clue: It's located in your house.

3) What's the cruelest thing you'll ever find a cook doing?
   Clue: It involves doing something with eggs and cream.

4) When does a person become a country in South America?
   Clue: It's the opposite of when you get hot (but find another word for cold). This word is the name of the country.

5) Which is heavier, a half or a full moon? Why?
   Clue: The opposite of "heavy" is "light." Think of how "light" has a double meaning.

6) What do liars to after they die?
   Clue: Think of a way to say, "They continue to lie" and "They don't move" in three words. ("They lie _____.")

PUNchline

7) What has four wheels and flies?
   Clue: Think of another meaning of "flies." This thing also doesn't smell very good.

8) When is a boy like a pony?
   Clue: Think of another way of saying "pony."

9) What flowers are the most kissable?
   Clue: What part of the body do we kiss with?

10) When are boys most like bears?
    Clue: The answer has something to do with their feet.

11) What goes around a button?
    Clue: This one is tricky. Close your eyes and say the words "a button" several times.

12) What kind of berry does every river contain?
    Clue: It's small and dark, and often a little sour. You're most likely to find it in jellies or jams.

13) What kind of fruit is found on every coin?
    Clue: It starts with a "d."

14) What has eyes but cannot see?
    Clue: It's a kind of vegetable.

15) When is an ear of corn like a question?
    Clue: What kind of corn do we eat when we go to the movies?
    Extra Clue: Familiar phrase used to refer to asking someone to marry you.

Words Within a Word

1) Everything is more expensive these days. You have to admit that a buccaneer is a very _____ for corn.
   Clue: If you paid a dollar for an ear of corn, wouldn't that be expensive?

2) What kind of key would be good to eat for dinner?
   Clue: Many eat them on a certain holiday.

3) What key is the most difficult to turn?
   Clue: It's another kind of animal.

4) What kind of ant is always a baby?
   Clue: It's a "kind" of person.

5) What room can no one enter?
   Clue: This room is actually a plant.

False Assumptions

1) Four friends walked to school under one umbrella. Why didn't any of them get wet?
   Clue: If you're under an umbrella, what do you assume? Was this really stated?

2) "Hey, did you hear about the new kid on the block? He does bird impressions. He eats _____."
   Clue: "Bird impression" usually refers to the sounds birds make, but what is a much more disgusting way to imitate a bird?

3) Name three things that contain milk other than butter and cheese.
   Answer: Ice cream, _____ and _____.
   Clue: The question doesn't really say "products" associated with milk, does it? Where does milk come from?

Familiar Phrases

1) What kind of weather do mice hate most?
   Clue: Think of a familiar phrase used to refer to a hard rain.

2) How did Jonah feel when the whale swallowed him?
   Clue: A phrase which means you're down or depressed. It has the word "mouth" in it.

Joking Answer Expected: True Answer Given

1) If you drop a white dress in the Black Sea, what does it become?
   Clue: What happens to anything when you put it into the water?

2) What question can never be answered by "Yes"?
   Clue: We often ask this question when we don't want to disturb someone.

3) Why does a chicken cross the road?
   Clue: This is a classic. No clue necessary, but just in case: Why does a person cross the road?

4) Why do people look over stone walls?
   Clue: None needed.

5) What do we have on Christmas day that we don't have any other day of the year?
   Clue: It's not something we eat or drink.

6) What kind of people usually go to heaven?
   Clue: What has to happen before anyone can go to heaven?

7) Why is it that when you lose something, you always find it in the last place you look?
   Clue: What do you do when you find it?

Misleading/Trick Questions

1) Which eat more grass, black sheep or white sheep?
   Clue: The question does not refer to the average black or white sheep.

2) What American has had the largest family?
   Clue: Think of another way of using the word "father." The answer is one of our Presidents.

3) When does water stop running down hill?
   Clue: There really is a circumstance in which water stops running down any hill.

4) How many pancakes could Goliath (the giant) eat on an empty stomach?
   Clue: Think about what it means to eat something on an empty stomach.

PUNchline

5) How far can you go into a forest?
   Clue: Don't think in terms of a particular distance. Think in terms of a percentage of the total distance from one side of the forest to the other side.

6) What has 18 legs, and catches flies?
   Clue: It's not an animal. It's a group of people. And "flies" has a double meaning.

7) On which side of country churches is the cemetery always located?
   Clue: The tricky part concerns the word "side."

8) When do cats have eight feet?
   Clue: Be careful about what you assume here. Pay special attention to the word "cats."

9) When a man falls, what does he fall against?
   Clue: The answer is not "the ground" (although it's a good answer). What do we say when we are forced to do something we don't really want to do?

10) Fashions change, but what's the one thing a person can always wear that's not out of style?
    Clue: It's something you do with a part of your body (your face).

Non-Joking Questions/Answers

1) What is yours, and yet used by others more than yourself?
   Clue: It's not a possession, or an object. It's actually a word.

2) What goes up, and never goes down?
   Clue: Again, it's not an object. But it's something all people have.

3) The more you take away from it, the larger it grows. What is it?
   Clue: You find it outside, in the ground.

4) A blind beggar had a brother, and the brother died. Yet the brother who died had no brother. How is that possible?
   Clue: You're making an assumption about the beggar that is not true.

5) If your uncle's sister is not your aunt, what relation is she to you?
   Clue: No clue needed here. There's only one other possibility.

6) What asks no questions, but requires many answers?
   Clue: It's a part of your house.

Nonsense

1) Why do chimneys smoke?
   Clue: "Because they can't _____." Think of another thing people often do that's not good for them.

2) What's purple, and hums?
   Clue: Many electric machines make a "humming" sound. The nonsense comes from the part that's purple. (You make wine from it.)

PUNchline

3) Why does it hum? (Refers to previous riddle.)
   Clue: Why do people sometimes hum songs?

Similarities

1) How is a bump like a hat?
   Clue: What are some hats made out of? (Sounds like "belt.")

2) How is your hand like a hardware store?
   Clue: What do we have on the end of our fingers?

3) What can you do to a piece of wood to make it like a king?
   Clue: Think of something we use to measure distances.

4) How is the sun like a loaf of white bread?
   Clue: Both rise, but the answer refers to what happens when they rise.

5) How are some old people like a window?
   Clue: It has to do with the fact that some old people say they "hurt all over." (This is also a pun.)

Differences

1) What's the difference between a boy with a cold and a smart boxer?
   Clue: Use the words "blow," "know," and "nose."

2) What's the difference between a donkey and a postage stamp?
   Clue: Use the words "stick" and "lick."

Children's Riddles and Jokes

3) What's the difference between a flea and a dog?
   Clue: The kind of answer here differs from the first two. Think about the fact that a dog "has" fleas.

4) What's the difference between a deer running away from hunters and a witch who's also a midget?
   Clue: Use the words "stag" and "hag."

5) What's the difference between a hungry man and a glutton?
   Clue: Use the words "eat" and "long."

ANSWERS TO CHILDREN'S RIDDLES AND JOKES

Puns

1) Time to get a new fence.
2) A carpet.
3) Beating eggs and whipping cream.
4) When he becomes Chili (chilly).
5) A half moon. Because a full moon is lighter (in the sense of being brighter, or giving off more light).
6) Still.
7) A garbage truck.
8) When he's a little hoarse (horse).
9) Tulips.
10) When they're in their bare (bear) feet.
11) A goat.
12) Currents.
13) Dates.
14) A potato.
15) When you pop it.

Words Within a Word

1) High price to pay (a "buck" an ear).
2) A turkey (tur-key).
3) A donkey (don-key).
4) An infant (inf-ant).
5) A mushroom.

False Assumptions

1) It wasn't raining.
2) "Worms."
3) Cows and goats.

Familiar Phrases

1) When it's raining cats and dogs.
2) He felt down in the mouth.

Joking Answer Expected: True Answer Given

1) Wet.
2) "Are you asleep?"
3) To get to the other side.
4) Because we can't see through them.

5) Christmas.
6) Dead people.
7) Because you stop looking when you find it.

Misleading/Trick Questions

1) White, because there are more of them.
2) George Washington, because he was the father of his country.
3) When it reaches the bottom of the hill.
4) One. After that his stomach wouldn't be empty.
5) Halfway (or to the center). After that, you're going out.
6) A baseball team.
7) The outside.
8) When there are two of them.
9) Against his will.
10) A smile.

Non-Joking Questions/Answers

1) Your name.
2) Your age.
3) A hole.
4) The beggar was a woman.
5) Your mother.
6) A doorbell.

PUNchline

Nonsense

1) Because they can't drink.
2) An electric grape.
3) Because it doesn't know the words.

Similarities

1) Both are felt.
2) Both have nails.
3) Make it into a ruler.
4) Both are light when they rise.
5) Because they're full of pains (panes).

Differences

1) One blows his nose, and the other knows his blows.
2) One you lick with a stick, and the other you stick with a lick.
3) A dog can have fleas, but a flea can't have dogs.
4) One's a hunted stag, and the other's a stunted hag.
5) One longs to eat and the other eats too long.

MIXED TYPES OF CHILDREN'S RIDDLES AND JOKES 2

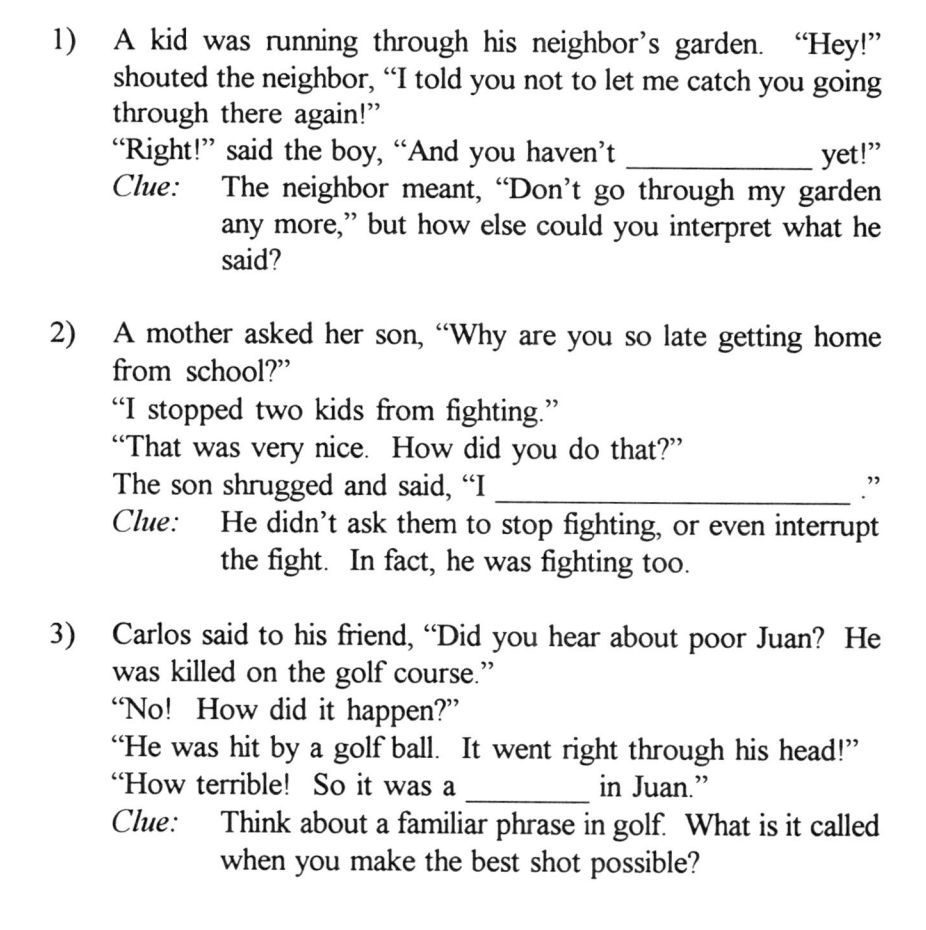

1) A kid was running through his neighbor's garden. "Hey!" shouted the neighbor, "I told you not to let me catch you going through there again!"
   "Right!" said the boy, "And you haven't _____ yet!"
   Clue: The neighbor meant, "Don't go through my garden any more," but how else could you interpret what he said?

2) A mother asked her son, "Why are you so late getting home from school?"
   "I stopped two kids from fighting."
   "That was very nice. How did you do that?"
   The son shrugged and said, "I _____."
   Clue: He didn't ask them to stop fighting, or even interrupt the fight. In fact, he was fighting too.

3) Carlos said to his friend, "Did you hear about poor Juan? He was killed on the golf course."
   "No! How did it happen?"
   "He was hit by a golf ball. It went right through his head!"
   "How terrible! So it was a _____ in Juan."
   Clue: Think about a familiar phrase in golf. What is it called when you make the best shot possible?

PUNchline

4) A woman walked into a sporting goods store and said, "I'd like a baseball bat for my son."
"I'm sorry," said the clerk, "we only sell bats; we don't _____ them."
Clue: Think about the word "for" here. How else could you interpret it?

5) If you're behind in a race, and you really want to win, what's the best food to eat?
Clue: Some people put this on french fries.

6) With what two animals do you always go to bed?
Clue: Actually, it's two of the same kind of animal. What part of your body has the name of an animal (when the animal is young)? It's in the lower part of your body.

7) When the clock strikes 13, what time is it?
Clue: It's not "one o'clock." If the clock strikes 13, there must be something wrong with it.

8) What is the smallest bridge in the world?
Clue: It's a part of your body.

9) What sticks up higher without the head than with the head?
Clue: You use it when you go to sleep.

10) Why don't women become bald as soon as men?
Clue: Think about the length of men's and women's hair.

11) What has four legs, but only one foot?
Clue: It's located in the bedroom.

12) Why isn't your nose 12 inches long?
Clue: What's another way of saying the length of something that's 12 inches long?

Mixed Types of Children's Riddles and Jokes

13) When is a man like a snake?
    Clue: What's the name of the snake that makes a sound when it shakes its tail?

14) What makes a road broad?
    Clue: Look carefully at the words "road" and "broad."

15) How many balls of string would it take to reach from the earth to the moon?
    Clue: The question says nothing about the length of the string.

16) A cat went into the basement with four feet, and came back with eight. How did he do that?
    Clue: He didn't grow four more feet.

17) How is a chicken sitting on a fence like a penny?
    Clue: How do we usually refer to the two sides of a coin?

18) What man shaves many times a day?
    Clue: Does the question say he's shaving himself?

19) What is full of holes, and yet holds water?
    Clue: What is good at "absorbing" water?

20) When is a black dog not a black dog?
    Clue: What dog has a color as part of its name?

21) Why would a donkey rather eat weeds than oats?
    Clue: What's another name for a donkey?

22) Who always goes to bed with their shoes on?
    Clue: It's not a person.

PUNchline

23) Why did the boy blush when he opened the refrigerator ?
    Clue: What do we put on salads?

24) Why couldn't they play cards on Noah's ark?
    Clue: Use the word "deck."

25) Which is most valuable, a silver dollar, or a paper dollar bill?
    Clue: You'll never guess this one. What happens when you fold a dollar bill?

26) When is a door not a door?
    Clue: How do we refer to a door that is open just a little bit?

27) If you go to the store to buy a dollar's worth of red tacks, what do you want them for?
    Clue: The answer does not refer to what you're going to do with them. What's another way of interpreting "want them for?"

28) What kind of cord is impossible to tie in a knot?
    Clue: It's not a kind of rope or string. Think of another way of interpreting the word "cord."

29) What driver will never get arrested for speeding?
    Clue: It's not a person. You may use this to fix things.

30) What weed (some call it a flower) belongs in a circus?
    Clue: It's a kind of lion.

31) How is snow like an oak tree?
    Clue: What happens to each in the spring?

Mixed Types of Children's Riddles and Jokes

32) I have a slender body and a tiny eye, and no matter what happens, I never cry. What am I?
   Clue: I'm an object used by people who make clothes.

33) What goes uphill and downhill, but never moves?
   Clue: It sounds like "toad."

34) What falls very often, but never gets hurt?
   Clue: Think about the weather.

35) What kind of pen should you never try to write with?
   Clue: You never find this pen in the city.

36) Did you hear about the cannibal who had a wife and _____ children?
   Clue: What number of children is consistent with the idea that he's a cannibal?

37) What two flowers do people always have with them?
   Clue: Both are located somewhere on your face.

38) What did the Spanish Fire Chief name his new twin sons? Jose and _____ B.
   Clue: Remember, he's Spanish. This is a pun. So think about the sound of "Jose," and the fact that he's a fireman.

ANSWERS TO MIXED CHILDREN'S RIDDLES AND JOKES

1) "Caught me."
2) "Beat them up."
3) "Hole" ("hole in one").
4) "Trade."
5) Catsup (Catch up).
6) Two calves.
7) Time to get a new clock.
8) The bridge of your nose.
   (It could also be a dental bridge in your mouth.)
9) A pillow.
10) Because they wear their hair longer.
11) A bed.
12) Because then it would be a foot.
13) When he gets rattled.
14) The letter "b."
15) One, if it's long enough.
16) He caught a mouse.
17) It's head is on one side, and its tail is on the other.
18) A barber.
19) A sponge.
20) A greyhound.

PUNchline

21) Because he's an ass.
22) Horses.
23) Because he saw the salad dressing.
24) Because there were too many animals on the deck.
25) A paper dollar, because when you put it in your wallet you double it, and when you take it out later, you can see it in creases.
26) When it's ajar.
27) A dollar.
28) A cord of wood.
29) A screw driver.
30) A dandelion.
31) Each leaves in the spring.
32) A needle.
33) A road.
34) Snow (or rain).
35) A pig pen.
36) Ate.
37) Tulips and iris.
38) "Hose B."

PUNS 3

1) A handsome young man invited his beautiful Chinese date up to his apartment to see his stamp collection as they left the movie theater. He told her he found her very attractive, intelligent, and talented. The girl smiled, shook here head "no," and said, "_____ will get you nowhere."
   Clue: Think of the familiar phrase women use when reacting to a compliment. Also, what is the name given to stamp collecting?
   The fact that she's Chinese adds a little something extra.

2) A psychiatrist who strongly believes in the notion of a "collective unconscious" complains that he always has trouble getting served in bars. All the bar tenders say I'm just too _____.
   Clue: What early follower of Freud believed in a collective unconscious? His first name is Karl.

3) Sign in front of a "Body and Fender Repair Shop:" "May we have the next _____?"
   Clue: Play with a formerly familiar phrase from ball rooms.

4) When the nudist colony opened just outside town, everyone expected a great deal of media attention, but there was very little _____.
   Clue: A familiar word used by the mass media.

PUNchline

5) An elephant in the jungle was drinking at the edge of a river when he spotted a snapping turtle asleep on a log. He ambled over and kicked it all the way across the river. "Why did you do that?" asked a giraffe standing nearby.
"Because," said the elephant, "I recognized it as the same turtle that took a nip at my trunk 20 years ago."
"What a memory!" said the giraffe in admiration.
"Yes, being an elephant, I have _____ recall."
Clue: They say an elephant never forgets. Play with the sound of the word that goes before "recall."

6) Show me a metal worker who knows how to make the hardware for bathrooms, and I'll show you a man who knows how to forge _____.
Clue: Make progress.

7) What kind of people were retread tires made for? People who were old enough to _____.
Clue: What do people generally do when they get to their middle sixties?

8) When Europeans first discovered how to make expresso coffee, everyone was very excited about the stimulating new taste. All agreed that this gave them _____ for a big celebration.
Clue: What's the term we use to refer to the by-product of making coffee?

9) A lady caused a big uproar recently when she brought her toy poodle with her while attending a flea circus. The poodle stole _____.
Clue: What's the usual association between dogs and fleas?

Puns

10) What kind of degree do they give dogs who successfully complete dog-training school?
    _____ degrees.
    Clue: Play with the term used for college degrees.

11) A man was locked in a room and told he couldn't come out until he made a pun. He immediately shouted, "_____ the door!" When he came out, he angrily quipped that anyone caught violently forcing others to create puns ought to be sentenced to do time in a _____.
    Clue: What's the natural word to use here (first blank)?

12) Oliver Wendell Holmes once said that as a physician, he was grateful for small _____.
    Clue: A play on a familiar phrase.
    What do we use thermometers for?

13) Two ropes walked into a fine restaurant. The waiter asked the first rope, "Are you one of them ropes?"
    "Why yes," stammered the rope.
    "Well, we don't serve your kind," said the waiter, as he threw him out.
    The second rope decided he'd better disguise himself, so he tied himself into a knot, and made his two ends all ragged. The waiter then walked over and said, "How about you, are you one of them ropes?"
    "I'm a _____," said the rope.
    Clue: It's a way of saying "no," but of describing what he's just done to himself, as well.

14) Zsa Zsa Gabor once remarked that, in spite of everyone's image of her, she really is a good housekeeper. In fact, every time she gets divorced, she _____.
    Clue: Be literal.

25

PUNchline

15) A well known singer was tired of singing alone all the time, but he could never get a partner to agree to join him. Finally, he solved the problem by going out and buying a _____.

   Clue: What do we generally buy when we don't want to pay someone else to do something? What's the term for two people singing together?

16) We all pitied the poor cow that tried to jump over a barbed wire fence. It was a(n) _____ disaster.
   Clue: A familiar phrase, which also refers to the part of the cow that milk comes from.

17) A friend of mine says he's tried every diet imaginable, but nothing has worked. Now he says, "I'm on a seafood diet. Every time I _____ food, I eat it."
   Clue: None needed.

18) Doctor to teenage girl (putting his stethoscope to his ears): "Big breaths."
   Patient: "Yeth, and I'm not even _____."
   Clue: The key is the word "yeth." She always talks this way.

19) When do doctors get most annoyed?
   When they're out of _____.
   Clue: Who do doctors treat?

20) What do you call a cow that's just delivered it's offspring? _____.

   Clue: Think of a kind of coffee. What kind do you drink if you're concerned about the harmful effects of coffee?

Puns

21) Did you hear about the (fill in the name of any group you want to put down) who took his wife to Domino's Pizza when she went into labor? He heard they had _____.
    Clue: What service did Domino's Pizza pioneer?

22) What's the best Christmas gift for the person who has everything? _____.
    Clue: Find another interpretation of "has everything." In this case, having everything is not good.

23) Why wouldn't the skeleton cross the road?
    He didn't have the _____.
    Clue: A familiar phrase meaning "didn't have the courage."

24) How can a pitcher win a baseball game without ever throwing a ball? By _____.
    Clue: He really does throw a ball . . . and yet he doesn't.

25) A father looked outside and saw his own children and their playmates pressing their hands into the cement of his newly laid sidewalk.
    He ran to the door and angrily gave the kids a real tongue-lashing.
    His shocked wife asked, "Don't you love your children?"
    He answered, "In the abstract, yes; but not in _____."
    Clue: Another word for what sidewalks are made of.

26) A photographer went into a haunted castle determined to get a photo of a ghost that was said to appear only once in a hundred years. Not wanting to frighten off the ghost, he waited in the dark until midnight, when the apparition appeared. The ghost turned out to be very friendly, and consented to pose for one

27

PUNchline

photo. The happy photographer popped a bulb into his camera and took the picture. He discovered later in his studio that the photo was underexposed and completely blank. So the _____ was willing, but the _____ was weak.
Clue: A familiar phrase about yielding to temptation.

27) A shipwrecked sailor was captured by cannibals. Each day, the natives would cut his arm with a dagger and drink some of his blood. Finally, he asked to see the king: "Look," he said, "if you're going to kill me and eat me, go ahead, but I'm sick and tired of getting _____ for the drinks."
Clue: The person who pays for everyone in a bar.

28) A man said he'd recently bought a _____ house. "The real-estate broker told me one story before I bought it, and another story afterward.
Clue: A house with two floors.

29) (My favorite joke from my high school years.) Three native American women are sitting around a fire. The first, sitting on a bearskin, has a son who weighs 170 pounds. The second, sitting on a deerskin, has a son who weighs 130 pounds. The third, sitting on a hippopotamus hide, weighs 300 pounds. What famous theorem does this illustrate?
   The _____ on the _____ is equal to the _____ of the _____ on the other two _____.
Clue: Its the Pythagorean theorem.

30) A marine biologist recently discovered a way to enable porpoises to live forever. But this unfortunately required him to feed them a particular species of baby sea gulls every day — and these gulls were on the endangered species list. One night,

while driving home with a fresh load of baby gulls, he ran over a lion who was reposing in the middle of the highway, smoking a corncob pipe and reading a book.

A policeman witnessed this, and immediately arrested him for transporting _____ gulls across a _____ lion for _____ porpoises.

Clue: A multiple play on a familiar phrase. A driver really can be arrested for the underlying idea represented here. (This is admittedly corny, but a good way to finish this section.)

ANSWERS TO PUNS

1) "Philately."
2) Jung (young).
3) "Dents?"
4) Coverage.
5) "Turtle."
6) "Ahead."
7) Retire.
8) Grounds.
9) The whole show.
10) Barkalaureate.
11) "O-pun." Punitentiary.
12) Fevers.
13) "Frayed knot."
14) Keeps the house.
15) Duet-yourself kit.
16) Udder.
17) "See food."
18) "Thixteen."
19) Patients (patience).
20) Decaffeinated.
21) Free delivery.
22) Antibiotics.
23) Guts.

PUNchline

24) Throwing only strikes.
25) "The concrete."
26) Spirit . . . flash.
27) Stuck.
28) Two-story.
29) Squaw . . . hippopotamus . . . sons . . . squaws . . . hides
30) Under-age . . . staid . . . immortal.

JOKES

4

1) Q: Why are lawyers buried 20 feet deep?
   A: Because _____ they're good people.
   Clue: A familiar phrase meaning, "in their heart."

2) Lawyer to client: "Have you ever been up before this judge?"
   Client: "Well, I don't know, what _____
   _____?"
   Clue: Find another meaning of "be up before."

3) A woman wrote to a newspaper columnist, expressing concern about her 30-year-old daughter, and her roommate, who didn't seem to want to have anything to do with men. She asked, "Do you think they could be _____?"
   Clue: She's confused about the term "lesbian."

4) "Say, I heard Mrs. Cargle in Room 324 had triplets."
   "Yes . . . they say it happens once in 10,000 times."
   "Amazing! How does she find time to _____?"
   Clue: There is confusion about the meaning of "10,000 times."

5) What's the most frequently heard phrase at the surgeon's annual ball?
   "May I _____?"
   Clue: What do you say when you want to dance with someone else's dance partner?

PUNchline

6) A doctor made a terrible mistake, and left a sponge inside the patient after surgery. There were no side effects, except that the patient was always _____.
   Clue: What is the main property of a sponge?

7) What did the doctor say to the patient after removing his appendix? "That'll be enough _____."
   Clue: This is something you might say to a kid who makes a "wise crack."

8) "I'm getting to the age that my mind's starting to wander. But I guess I shouldn't worry, it can't _____."
   Clue: This is a put-down of oneself. If you weren't too bright, how would this influence the meaning of "wander?"

9) What is the oldest known form of oral contraception?
   Clue: Think about the ambiguity of the word "oral."

10) What do you call investors who wait around to buy up bankrupt firms?
    Clue: Come up with a variation of "venture capitalists." Change the word "venture."

11) What's the difference between a teacher and a railroad conductor?
    Clue: Use the words "train" and "mind."

12) They let commercial pilots start flying these days with almost no experience. Last week, the pilot of the plane I flew in was so new at the job that the plane had _____.
    Clue: How do kids learn to ride a bicycle?

13) (As a roast) In his long career, he has consistently done the work of two men, _____.
    Clue: Name two people who are known to be incompetent bunglers.

Jokes

14) A nurse just out of nursing school hadn't yet learned that the polite word for "bedpan" in this hospital was "vase." She was about to leave a male patient's room when he asked, "Nurse, would you bring me a vase right away?"
   "Sure, Mister Talbert," she said, "How big is your _____?"
   Clue: A natural error, if you don't know the hospital meaning of "vase." (But note the ambiguous meaning you're left with in this joke.)

15) During a period of heavy flooding in town, everyone was asked to get shots to prevent an outbreak of typhoid. The place residents had to go for their shots depended on their precinct. One woman, after showing her identification to the staff was told: "Lady, you'll have to get your shot in your precinct."
   "How come?" she asked. "All the others are getting their shots in their _____."
   Clue: She misunderstands "precinct."

16) When the doctor answered the phone, a frantic father was shouting, "Come quick, Doc, my little boy swallowed a condom!"
   The doctor hung up, grabbed his bag, and was running out the door when the phone rang again. "Never mind, Doc," said the boy's father, "I found _____."
   Clue: The concern was not for the boy's well being. Assume that the only concern here was sexual.

17) "Call me a cab!"
   "OK, _____."
   Clue: Look for a second meaning of a key word.

18) A man got his wife a toy poodle for her birthday. But she almost killed it trying to get the _____ into it.
   Clue: What's often missing from toys kids get for Christmas?

35

PUNchline

19) There was this guy whose conscience was bothering him because he cheated on his income tax. So he wrote a letter to IRS, and said, "Dear sir: Five years ago, I cheated on my income tax. I haven't been able to sleep a wink since. Enclosed, please find $500. If I still can't sleep, I'll _____ _____."

Clue: A remark which draws attention to something he really doesn't want to draw attention to.

20) "Doctor, my husband thinks he's a chicken."
"How long has this been going on?"
"About five years."
"Well why haven't you brought him in sooner?"
"Well, to tell you the truth, up til now, we needed _____."

Clue: The husband is not the only one who has the delusion.

21) Obstetricians' motto: "Always at your _____."

Clue: Wordplay on a part of the anatomy.

22) A doctor calls in a very anxious patient and says, "I'm afraid I have bad news and worse news. The bad news is that your tests were positive, and you have 24 hours to live."

"Good Lord!" said the patient, "What could be worse?"

"The worse news," said the doctor, "is that I got the results _____ and _____."

Clue: What would lead the patient to have even less than 24 hours?

23) What do we mean by "paradox?"

Clue: Make three words out of this word.

24) The gynecologist looked up after completing his examination. "I'm sorry, miss, but removing that vibrator is going to involve a lengthy and delicate operation."

36

Jokes

"I'm not sure I can afford it," sighed the woman. "Why don't you just replace _____?"
Clue: If it's to expensive to remove, she may as well get some use out of it while it's there.

25) A man is in the hospital to have his gangrene-infected leg amputated. He wakes up after the operation, and asks, "How'm I doin' doc?"
"Well, I've got some good news, and some bad news. The bad news is that we amputated the wrong leg."
"My god! I can't believe it," says the patient. "What's the good news?"
"Your other leg _____."
Clue: No clue necessary.

26) Think of another way to say, "The sausage has not yet arrived."
"The _____ is yet to _____."
Clue: Start with a German word which means sausage. It's a phrase you've heard before.

27) Did you hear about the two angels who got kicked out of heaven? They were trying to _____ a _____.
Clue: This is a double pun.
Find a phrase which means to make money.

28) Item on news broadcast. "The Detroit Police Department reported today that someone broke into Police Headquarters during the night and damaged their toilet facilities. The sabotage remains a mystery, and at present the police have nothing to _____."
Clue: No clue necessary.

29) Why did the elephants quit their job at the factory?
They got tired of working for _____.
Clue: They were underpaid.

37

PUNchline

30) Did you hear about the tomcat who ate cheese so he could look down rat holes with _____ breath?
Clue: What do we use minnows for, when fishing?

31) An Iowa farmer visits his cousin in New York. They come out of a restaurant and find it raining. "Oh no," said the farmer, "It's raining cats and dogs. It's the worse thing that could happen during my visit."
"Oh, there's something worse than that," said the New Yorker, "_____ taxis."
Clue: Calling taxis. A familiar weather-related term.

32) What do you call a clairvoyant midget running from the law?
A _____ at _____.
Clue: Use the names of the three traditional clothing sizes.

33) "I have a delicious piece of gossip to tell you, but listen carefully. I can only tell it once, because I promised that I wouldn't _____."
Clue: The understanding was not to tell anyone, but technically, the person can tell it once, because the agreement was to not _____ it.

34) A harried resident was walking down the hospital corridor when a nurse stopped him. "Dr. Thomas," she whispered, "you've got a thermometer stuck behind your ear."
"Hell!" he yelled. "Some _____ has my pen."
Clue: Where are thermometers sometimes placed?

35) An elderly woman, assumed to be unconscious, is wheeled into the emergency room. The paramedic says, "She's critical." The woman opens her eyes and says, "_____."
Clue: How might she react to the "other" meaning of "critical?"

Jokes

36) How many Yuppies does it take to change a light bulb? Two. One to mix the _____, and one to call _____.
    Clue: Would a Yuppie do it him/herself?

37) Why are surgeons funnier than other doctors? Because they keep their patients _____.
    Clue: Another way of saying they keep their patients laughing.

38) A German had to have surgery while visiting the U.S. The doctor asked if he wanted a local anesthetic. He said, "Well, I'd really prefer a _____ one."
    Clue: The key word is "local." Remember, the patient comes from another country.

39) A patient asked the doctor why his lower back was always stiff as a board. "Well, that's not surprising," said the doctor, "that's the _____ region of your back."
    Clue: What the name of the place you go to get two-by-fours and other large pieces of wood?

40) An unfortunate five-year-old girl got very sick after swallowing a nickel, two dimes, and three pennies. The doctors treated her for weeks, but there was _____.
    Clue: She didn't improve.

41) "Our next speaker is tall, dark, and handsome. Wait, I misread that. He's tall and, in the _____, handsome."
    Clue: No clue needed here.

42) "I'd like to introduce the entire panel to you. From right to left, and this is not a _____ . . ."
    Clue: Find another way to interpret "right to left."

PUNchline

43) I know a clothing salesman who has a hundred suits, and they're all _____.
   Clue: Look for a legal meaning of the word "suit."

44) "Order! Order in the court!"
   "_____, please, your Honor."
   Clue: Look for a simple pun here.

45) A man asked a lawyer what his fee was.
   "Fifty dollars for three questions," said the lawyer.
   "That's pretty steep, isn't?"
   "Yes. Now what's your _____?"
   Clue: He's a lawyer, so you'd better take him literally.

46) There's a gate separating heaven and hell. One day it gets knocked down, and St. Peter goes to examine the damage. He calls the devil and says, "The gate's down again. It's your turn to fix it."
   "Forget it," says the devil, "my people are much too busy."
   "But we had a deal," says St. Peter, "and if you don't honor it, we'll sue you for breach of contract."
   "Right," says the devil, "and just where are you going to find a _____?"
   Clue: No clue needed.

47) Two mice are chatting in a laboratory: "And how are you getting along with your professor?"
   "Oh, great! Every time I _____, he _____."
   Clue: Think about Pavlov and his conditioned dogs.

48) Did you hear about the angel who got kicked out of heaven for trying to make a _____.
   Clue: You've already seen this joke. What is the main motive of a capitalist?

49) He's not much of a musician. He doesn't even know the difference between _____ and Acapulco.
Clue: A way of singing.

50) Where do you get dragon milk? From cows with _____.
Clue: Play with the sound of "dragon."

51) What do you get if you cross a dog and a chicken?
_____ eggs.
Clue: Combine a familiar word for "dog" with a way of preparing eggs to eat.

52) What do you get when you cross an owl and a pig?
Clue: An owl seems to stare at you. Pigs like to wallow in dirt and mud.

53) How many flies does it take to screw in a light bulb?
Clue: None given, even though you may need one.

54) What to you get when you cross a bale of straw with an octopus?
Clue: A strange sweeping device.

55) What do you get when you cross a parrot with a hyena?
Clue: What is each species known for?

56) What do you get when you cross a woodpecker with a carrier pigeon?
Clue: How do you know when a carrier pigeon arrives?

57) What do you get when you cross a robin and a ball point pen?
Clue: What is an important feature of many ball point pens? A feature you use when you're through writing?

PUNchline

58) What do you get when you cross a hippopotamus with a peanut butter sandwich?
   Clue: What happens to your mouth when you eat a peanut butter sandwich?

59) What do you get when you cross an elephant with the family dog?
   Clue: This is not a typical cross joke. Think about the stereotypic relationship between mailmen and dogs.

60) How are a duck and an icicle alike?
   They both grow _____.
   Clue: Think of ski jackets known for their warmth.

61) "It's raining cats and dogs outside."
   "I know, I just stepped in a _____."
   Clue: Take what's left on the ground after it rains, and change the sound so that it becomes the name of a small indoor dog.

62) A man walks into a bar in a tough neighborhood, and asks, "What do you have on ice?" The bartender says, "You wouldn't know ____."
   Clue: What else might be put on ice or in another cool place in a tough neighborhood? (Actually, this is generally done in a morgue.)

63) What's the difference between an elephant and a jar of peanut butter?
   The elephant doesn't _____.
   Clue: You probably know this. Its the classic elephant joke.

Jokes

64) Q: What do Hiroshima, Nagasaki, and Baghdad have in common? (Joke circulating during the war with Iraq.)
A: _____.
Clue: Yes, it has something to do with nuclear bombs, but find some way of adding an unexpected twist to the answer.

65) Q: What's today's weather forecast for Baghdad? (Another joke circulating during the war with Iraq.)
A: Cloudy and windy, with temperatures in the _____.
Clue: There were rumors of the possibility of dropping a "limited" nuclear bomb on Baghdad.

66) My wife's really not too bright. She went shopping last week, and someone stole the car while she was in the store. I asked her, "Did you see what he looked like?" She said, "No but I got _____."
Clue: An observation that's generally helpful, but not when it's your own car.

67) A tailor was robbed, and the police asked if he could describe the guy. He said, "Of course I can, he was a _____."
Clue: What terms do tailors use on their jobs?

68) "I just saw a man-eating shark in the aquarium!"
"Big deal! I just saw a man-eating _____ in the restaurant."
Clue: Look for a second interpretation of "man-eating shark."

69) My mother just got a new job. She's a travel agent for guilt _____.
Clue: Something stereotypically associated with Jewish mothers.

PUNchline

70) After years of research, scientists have finally concluded that the fetus becomes viable after _____.
    Clue: This is impossible to guess, but will be appreciated by parents with adult children living at home.

71) A father tells his teenage daughter, "There are two words I'd like to you drop from your vocabulary. One is 'awesome,' and the other is 'gross'."
    "OK," she said, "What _____?"
    Clue: Think of a second way of interpreting what the father is saying. The daughter doesn't realize that he's talking about dropping these two specific words.

72) Why did the cookie cry?
    Because it's mother had been a _____ so long.
    Clue: Its a kind of cookie. This is a children's joke.

73) My daughter thinks I'm too nosy. At least that's what she scribbles in her _____.
    Clue: The one place that shows that her daughter is right.

74) In my teens, my mother always said, "The way you put things off, you'll never amount to anything."
    I said, "Oh yeah, just _____."
    Clue: Technically, this shows his mother was right.

75) As two politicians discuss strategies, the Democrat says, "Whenever I take a cab, I give the driver a large tip and say, 'Vote Democratic'."
    The Republican says, "I have a similar approach. Whenever I take a cab, I _____, and say, 'Vote Democratic'."
    Clue: Remember, this is a Republican talking, so if he says the same thing as the Democrat, is he doing the same thing with the driver?

Jokes

76) The controversy about giving aid to the Contras in Nicaragua in the 1980s has finally been resolved. When President Reagan made a favorable statement about "contraceptives," Ollie North misunderstood him, thinking he said _____."
    Clue: Turn the word "contraceptives" around.

77) Did you hear about Ronald Reagan's new fast-food chicken franchise in California? They only serve _____ wings.
    Clue: What's the classic distinction between conservative and liberal politics?

78) What would it take to legalize marijuana these days? A _____ session of congress.
    Clue: You probably don't need a clue for this.

79) What do Saddam Hussein and his father have in common? Neither one _____ in time.
    Clue: Find a sexual link.

80) How can you tell when a politician is lying? His lips _____.
    Clue: A stereotypic view of politicians.

81) They're finally getting around to putting a clock on the Leaning Tower of Pisa. Now they'll have both the time and the _____ _____.
    Clue: Plays on a familiar phrase, in which one has the time, but does not want to do something.

82) Two women walk into a club for men only. The waiter comes over and says, "I'm sorry ladies, but we only serve men here." One of the women answers, "Oh good, _____ _____."
    Clue: The key word is serve.

45

PUNchline

83) Two lawyers (put your favorite victim here) were out walking in the woods when they came upon a set of tracks. One lawyer said, "Those are wolf tracks." The other said, "no, they're bear tracks." Just then, they both looked up and got hit by a _____.

Clue: They were both wrong. They were hit by something moving 60 mph.

84) A man tells his psychiatrist, "It was terrible. I was in Europe on business, and I wired my wife that I'd be back a day early. I rushed home from the airport and found her in bed with my best friend. How could she do this to me?"
    The psychiatrist pauses reflectively, and says, "Well, maybe she _____."
Clue: The psychiatrist is not giving the support the client expects. But his answer does make sense in another way.

85) How many psychiatrists does it take to screw in a light bulb? Only one, but the bulb must really _____.
Clue: Psychiatrists help people change their behavior. But what is usually the first step?

86) Native American to psychiatrist: "I don't know what it is, Doc, some days I feel like a tee pee, and some days I feel like a wig wam."
    Psychiatrist: "You know what your problem is? You're two _____."
Clue: He's anxious.

87) During an interview of Winston Churchill on his 87th birthday, a reporter said, "Sir Winston, I hope to wish you well on your 100th birthday." Churchill quipped, "_____."
Clue: There's a turning of the tables here regarding the focus of the reporter's comments.

Jokes

88) A farmer called the fire department, yelling excitedly: "This is Dave Van Nuck. My barn is on fire. Get out here as quick as you can!"
"Ok," said the dispatcher, "but how do we get there?"
Dave paused a moment, and said, "Don't you have those _____ any more?"
Clue: The word "how" is ambiguous.

89) President Lincoln was once asked if the press reports regarding a particular issue were reliable. He is said to have answered, "First they _____, and then they re- _____, so I guess that makes them reliable."
Clue: Again, find a second way of interpreting a key word here.

90) A woman who wanted to improve her self-concept went to a bookstore and asked the manager where the _____ section was. The manager said, "If I told you, that would defeat the whole purpose."
Clue: The joke itself contains all the clues you need (but you will need to think about it a bit).

91) When Victor Borge was asked why the keys of his piano were so yellow, he insisted that it was not because the piano was old. It was because "the elephant _____."
Clue: What causes yellowing in humans?

92) The rape victim was brought into the room, and one man in the police lineup spotted her and said, "That's _____ right!"
Clue: There's a kind of reversal operating here.

93) The butcher was waiting on a woman when Mrs. Bottleson rushed in and said, "Give me a pound of cat food, quick!"

PUNchline

　　　Turning to the other customer, who had been waiting for some time, Mrs. Bottleson said: "I hope you don't mind my getting waited on before you."
　　　"Not if you're that _____," quipped the other customer.
　　　Clue:　The implication is that she's not getting the cat food for her cat.

94)　"My wife and I were happy for 25 years."　"Then what happened?"
　　　"We _____."
　　　Clue:　Does it really say they had 25 happy years of marriage?

95)　Two women are talking.　"Do you ever wake up grouchy?"
　　　"No, I usually _____."
　　　Clue:　Look for a second interpretation of "wake up."

96)　A wife playfully says to her husband, "You need a self-starter to get you up in the morning." Her husband answers grouchily, "Oh no I don't. Not with a _____ like you around."
　　　Clue:　A hostile response. How were the earliest cars started?

97)　"I understand your mother-in-law is very ill."
　　　"That's right. In fact, she's in the hospital."
　　　"I'm sorry to hear that. How long has she been in the hospital?"
　　　"Well, in three weeks, it'll be _____."
　　　Clue:　He doesn't like his mother-in-law.

98)　A man who always has bad luck with the ladies decides to try a more assertive approach. He sees an attractive woman in a bar, buys her a drink, chats a while, then smiles, and with a wink, drops his hotel room key into her purse. He waits an hour, for the sake of appearances, and then goes back to his room. His luggage _____.
　　　Clue:　There was no suggestion that the woman reacted positively to him.

Jokes

99) Trying to talk to him is like trying to take a sip out of a _____.

   Clue: Exaggerate! Find a situation involving water where it's impossible to take a sip.

100) Woman to her husband: "Honey, the car is _____."
   Husband: "How do you know?"
   Wife: "Because its in the swimming pool."
   Clue: None needed.

101) A man known by everyone in the church to be a heavy drinker asks Father O'Mally what scoliosis is. The priest, thinking that this is a good chance to teach him a lesson, says, "Scoliosis is a condition caused by too much drinking and carousing! Why do you ask? Do you have it bad?"
   "Oh no Father," answered the man, I was just reading in the paper that _____ has it."
   Clue: How can you make this embarrassing to the priest, given what he just said?

102) Little Bobby swallowed a penny.
   "Quick," shouted his mother, "Call a doctor!"
   "Doctor, schmocter!" shouted his father. "Call the rabbi. He can get _____ out of _____!"
   Clue: Think more broadly than this particular penny.

103) How do you convert a "man of gold" into a "man of God?"
   "Knock the _____ out of him."
   Clue: Look at the words "gold" and "God." How do they differ?

104) What did the agnostic dyslexic have to say about religion?
   "There is no _____!"
   Clue: What would he say about God?

PUNchline

105) Why didn't the Maharishi accept novocaine when he went to the dentist? Because he prefers to transcend _____.
Clue: What kind of meditation did the Maha-rishi Mahesh Yogi do? Play with the term used for this meditation.

106) "Operator, this is Reverend Thomas in Boston. I'd like to place a call to Reverend Pearson in Los Angeles."
"Will you speak with anyone else who answers?"
"No, make it _____ to _____."
Clue: A particular kind of phone call which requires an operator's assistance (and think of another word for priest).

107) "_____! _____! _____!" said one monk to another. "Is that all you ever think about?"
Clue: It sounds just like a familiar phrase. What term do we use to refer to a religious group having views which differ from that of the parent organization?

108) Jim Baker has been writing a book based on his experiences in the late 1980s. It's called "Do clergy do more than _____ people?"
Clue: What do you call someone who is not associated with the church?

109) How many religious zealots does it take to change a light bulb?
Clue: Remember, God is omnipotent.

110) Catholic schools aren't always against sex education. A lot of them have sex education classes. The nuns teach that sex is a perfectly normal bodily event. Like a _____.
Clue: Name any clearly negative thing that might happen to one's body.

50

Jokes

111) How many Zen masters does it take to screw in a light bulb?
Two.   One to _____ and one not to _____.
Clue: Yin and Yang.

112) A 70-year-old woman went to see her doctor with the following complaint: "I don't know what it is doctor, I just don't seem to have the desire for sex that I used to have."
The doctor answered, "Well, that's understandable for a woman your age. When did you first notice this?"
"Well, _____."
Clue: Remember, the stereotype is that a 70-year-old woman has lost interest in sex. Exaggerate, in the opposite direction.

113) A father and his son were disappointed by the lethargy of the expensive bull they just bought. So they called in the vet, who came by while the son was at school. When he got home, his father told him that the vet had rubbed the bull's gums with a yellow ointment. And the bull, having kicked down his stall, was in the process of mating with every cow in the herd.
"Fantastic!" said the son. "What was in the ointment?"
"Don't know," said Pa, "but it had a vanilla _____."
Clue: It may take a minute to see this one. If it had that effect on the bull . . .

114) How do you tell the sex of a chromosome?
Pull down its _____.
Clue: Think of a variation of "Pull down its pants."

115) A friend of mind has discovered a new form of _____ contraception. When her boyfriend wants to have sex, she says, "No."
Clue: None needed.

PUNchline

116) Did you hear about the terrible way Pee Wee Herman died? From a massive _____.
    Clue: It's a sexual play on words. What results from a blood clot in the brain?

117) Do you know why Pee Wee Herman didn't bother hiring a lawyer? He knew he could get himself _____.
    Clue: Again, it's sexual.

118) Said Billy Rose to Sally Rand (a fan dancer in the 1930s), "Sally, dance without your fan."
    So Sally danced without her fan.
    Billy _____ and Sally _____.
    Clue: The word play is in their last names. Again, it's sexual.

119) Sign at Adam and Eve's house: "We're never _____."
    Clue: Play with the word used to indicate that you're open for business 24 hours a day.

120) Sign on front door of music store: "Gone _____, back in a _____."
    Clue: A play on a familiar phrase. Each missing word distorts a familiar word. Use the name of a famous composer (especially associated with the piano).

121) Pravda (Pre-Gorbachev) announced a contest in Moscow for the best political joke. First prize: _____.
    Clue: Political jokes in the pre-Gorbachev years were not very well-received by party leaders. So the answer must contain something negative.

122) An American tourist in Moscow (pre-Gorbachev) is explaining our democratic system: "An American can stand on the steps of the Capitol Building and shout: 'The President is a bum!'"

Jokes

The Russian says, "But we can do that too. Any Russian can stand on the steps at the Kremlin and shout: 'The _____ is a bum!'"
Clue: What the Russian is agreeing to is just the opposite of what you think he's agreeing to.

123) Soviet newspaper feature (pre-Gorbachev): "Believe it or _____."
Clue: A play on Ripley's "Believe it or not." Remember, there was no choice but to accept the Party line.

124) Did you hear that NASA has established a new restaurant on the moon? It has great food, and low prices, but no _____.
Clue: Think of another way to say "The ambience is poor."

125) A man lost 82 straight bets in trying to pick winners in pro football games. "Why not try hockey?" asked his friend.
"Hockey?" he answered, "I don't _____ hockey."
Clue: The logic behind the answer is inconsistent with the fact that he's lost his last 82 bets on football.

126) A woman was fired from her job at a frozen orange juice company. They said she just couldn't _____.
Clue: What term do we use to refer to the nature of the orange juice when it's frozen?

127) Why do cannibals refuse to eat clowns? Because they taste _____.
Clue: A word which implies "bad," but has an extra meaning here.

128) (A Classic) "Waiter, what's this fly doing in my soup?"
"Well, I don't know, sir, but it looks like _____."
Clue: The key word here is "doing."

53

PUNchline

129) "Waiter, what is this you've served me?"
"Why that's _____ soup, sir."
"I'm not interested in what it's _____. I want to know what it is now!"
Clue: Only one kind of soup makes a joke out of this.

130) What do you get when you cross a toaster with an electric blanket?
Clue: What do a lot of people have difficulty doing in the morning when they wake up? And what is a prominent feature of toasters?

131) What do you get when you cross a freeway with a bicycle?
Clue: This joke violates the usual pattern of cross jokes. If you wanted to trick someone after a series of cross jokes, what answer might you give here? Treat "cross" as a pun.

132) What does a grape say when you step on it?
Nothing. It just gives a little _____.
Clue: Think of a young child who's upset.

133) How do you get down from an elephant?
You don't _____.
Clue: Find an answer based on a pun here.

134) How can you tell when an elephant is getting ready to charge?
He takes out his _____.
Clue: No clue necessary. Many elephant jokes follow this formula.

135) A (fill in any country you want to victimize) airplane lands on the runway with great difficulty. As they taxi, the pilot says, "My God! That's the shortest runway I've ever seen!"

54

Jokes

"You're not kidding," says the co-pilot, looking out his window. "But it sure is _____."
Clue: If its a normal airport, what kind of absurd confusion is possible here?

136) May your future happiness and success be like Ireland's capital — always _____.
Clue: Increasing. What is Ireland's capital?

137) What do you call a dude in the Navy? _____.
Clue: Use the word for underwater boats. Think of a word which means "emotionally down."

138) "Did you ever see the Catskill Mountains?"
"No, but I've seen them _____."
Clue: No clue necessary.

139) "What happened to Johnny when he fell through the screen door?"
"He got a _____ muscle."
Clue: What are screens sometimes used for?

140) What's the difference between a cat and a comma?
A cat has _____ at the end of its _____, and a comma has a _____ at the end of its _____.
Clue: The two key words both sound like "flaws."

141) A concerned Mr. Goldfarb tells his wife that the doctor said he'd contracted a bad case of gonorrhea. His wife goes to the dictionary and looks the word up.
"Not to worry," she says, "it says right here that it's an inflammation of the _____."
Clue: She misunderstood a key word. Remember, she's Jewish.

55

PUNchline

142) An elderly man with a hearing problem suddenly goes deaf in one ear. He goes to a doctor, who pulls a suppository out of his ear. "Here's the trouble," says the doctor.
  The old man sighs in relief. "Now I know what I did with my _____."
  Clue: There's only one possible source of confusion here for someone who's hard of hearing.

143) Why do (fill in any nationality you want to put down) doctors always make lousy lovers?
  They always wait for the _____ to go down.
  Clue: A familiar phrase used in connection with certain injuries.

144) An elderly senator told his hot-bodied young bride, "Baseball season starts tomorrow and I've been asked to throw out the first ball."
  She retorted, "For all the good you've done me lately, you might as well throw them _____ out."
  Clue: She's not happy with her sex life.

145) "I hear the President's wife is gonna ask for a divorce."
  "Really? Why?"
  "She claims he's not _____ what he's doing to the country."
  Clue: It's sexual. It's also a negative statement about how he's leading the country.

146) Friend: "How'd you come out in the argument with your wife?"
  Husband: "Oh, she came crawling to me on hands and knees."
  Friend: "Is that so?"
  Husband: "Yes." She said, "Come out from _____ _____."
  Clue: He's being literal, and he lost the argument.

56

Jokes

147) My wife and I have our differences. But, like a Californian after an earthquake, we always say, "With all your _____, I love you still."
   Clue: Where in California do earthquakes occur?

148) A nudist camp tried to recruit new members by advertising a special: "Only _____ for new members."
   Clue: Play with a familiar phrase used in sales. But remember, it's a nudist camp.

149) A visitor to New Mexico was struck by how dry everything looked. "Don't you ever get any rain here?" he asked a local. The resident thought, and then asked, "Do you remember the story about Noah and the Ark, and how it rained for 40 days and 40 nights?"
   "Of course I do," said the visitor.
   "Well that time, we _____."
   Clue: The technique used here is exaggeration (in a negative direction).

150) Bumper sticker: Old mailmen never die. They just lose their _____.
   Clue: Synonym for zest or energy.

ANSWERS TO JOKES

1) Deep down.
2) "Time does he get up?"
3) "Lebanese?"
4) "Get her work done?"
5) "Cut in?"
6) Thirsty.
7) "Out of you."
8) "Go far."
9) The word "no."
10) Vulture capitalists.
11) One trains the mind, and the other minds the train.
12) Training wheels.
13) Laurel and Hardy.
14) "Bouquet?"
15) "Arm."
16) "Another one."
17) "You're a cab."
18) Batteries.
19) "Send you the rest."
20) "The eggs."
21) "Cervix."
22) "Yesterday and forgot to call."

23) Two doctors.

24) "The batteries?"

25) "Is getting better."

26) "The worst is yet to come."

27) Make a prophet (profit).

28) "Go on."

29) For peanuts.

30) Baited.

31) "Hailing."

32) Small medium at large.

33) "Repeat."

34) "Asshole."

35) "I am not! You're doing fine."

36) The drinks . . . the electrician.

37) In stitches.

38) "German (or European)."

39) "Lumbar."

40) No change.

41) "Dark"

42) "Political statement"

43) Pending.

44) "A cheeseburger and fries" (or another food order).

45) "Third question?"

46) "Lawyer?"

47) "Ring the bell . . . brings me food."

Jokes

48) Prophet?
49) Acapella.
50) Short legs.
51) Pooched.
52) A bird that gives you dirty looks.
53) Two. The question is, how did they get in there?
54) A broom with eight handles.
55) An animal that can tell you what it's laughing at.
56) A bird that knocks on the door when it delivers the message.
57) A robin with a retractable beak.
58) A hippo that sticks to the roof of your mouth.
59) A very nervous mailman.
60) Down.
61) "Poodle."
62) "Him."
63) Stick to the roof of your mouth.
64) Nothing . . . yet.
65) Upper twenty thousands (or any other number suggesting a nuclear bomb).
66) "The license number."
67) "38-short, let out the shoulders and take in the waist."
68) "Herring (or other fish commonly served in a restaurant)."
69) Trips.
70) Seven months of continuous employment.
71) "Are they?"
72) Wafer.

PUNchline

73) Diary.
74) "Wait."
75) "I don't give any tip at all."
76) "Receptive contras."
77) "Right."
78) Joint.
79) Pulled out.
80) Are moving.
81) Inclination.
82) "Bring us two, please" ("two to go," etc.).
83) Train
84) "Didn't get your telegram."
85) Want to change.
86) "(Too) tents."
87) "You might make it, you look healthy."
88) "Red trucks."
89) "Lie . . . relie."
90) Self-help.
91) "Smoked too much."
92) "Her all."
93) "Hungry."
94) "Met (or got married)."
95) "Let him sleep."
96) "Crank."
97) "A month."
98) Was gone.

Jokes

99) Fire hydrant.
100) Flooded.
101) "The Pope."
102) "Money . . . anybody."
103) "L."
104) "Dog!"
105) Dental medication.
106) "Parson to parson."
107) "Sects! Sects! Sects!"
108) "Lay."
109) None. They just sit and wait for the Lord to change it.
110) Stroke (cancer, etc.).
111) Screw in the bulb (in each blank).
112) "Last night, and then again this morning."
113) "Taste."
114) "Genes."
115) Oral.
116) Stroke.
117) Off.
118) Rose . . . Ran(d).
119) "Clothed."
120) "Chopin . . . minuet."
121) 20 years.
122) "American President."
123) "Else."
124) Atmosphere.

PUNchline

125) "Know anything about."
126) Concentrate.
127) Funny.
128) "The back stroke."
129) "Bean." "Been (pronounced with a British accent)."
130) A blanket that pops you out of bed in the morning.
131) Killed.
132) Wine.
133) Get down from an elephant. You get down from a goose.
134) Credit card.
135) "Wide."
136) Dublin (doubling).
137) Sub dude.
138) "Kill mice."
139) "Strained."
140) "Claws . . . paws . . . pause . . . clause."
141) "Gentiles."
142) "Hearing aid."
143) Swelling.
144) "Both."
145) "Doing to her."
146) "Under that bed, you coward."
147) Faults.
148) "50% off."
149) "Got about an inch."
150) Zip.

STORIES AND LONGER JOKES 5

1) Herb is the lone survivor of a shipwreck, along with his dog. After two days clinging to a floating piece of wreckage, they come upon an island. The island is deserted, but has hundreds of sheep.

Herb has never been attracted to animals, but after a while he gets so lonely and frightened of dying that he finds himself looking longingly at one of the lambs. But as soon as he goes near her, his dog starts barking and chases the lamb away. The next morning, Herb can think of nothing but the lamb. He gets up early, sneaks over to the lamb, and just as he touches her, the dog again runs up yelping loudly, and scares her away.

A week later, Herb and the dog are walking along the beach, and come across a beautiful young woman lying unconscious on the sand. Herb rushes up and gives her mouth-to-mouth resuscitation, and after a while, she comes to. "Where am I? What happened?"

"You must have survived the shipwreck," he says. "You were unconscious, but I guess I got to you in time."

"Oh, I just don't know how I can thank you," she says, giving him a long tender kiss and pushing her body up against his. "Please let me show my appreciation to you in some way. Just tell me how I can please you. I'll do anything you want."

"Well," says Herb, "there _is_ something. Would you mind _____?"

Clue: If it's what he'd normally say here, it wouldn't be a joke. Think back to the rest of the story. What about the sheep?

PUNchline

2) A man in his 70s has a woman half his age fall hopelessly in love with him. He says, "I can't marry you, my dear. Father and mother are against it."

She's startled. "What? At your age, your parents are still living?"

"No," he explains, "I mean father _____ and mother _____."

Clue: Think of two familiar two-word expressions consistent with the idea that this marriage wouldn't work very well.

3) A boy is pulling his wagon down the street when the wheels fall off. "I'll be damned!" he says, and puts the wheels back on.

A couple of minutes later, the wheels fall off again. "I'll be damned!" says the boy, and puts them on again.

This time a clergyman overhears him. "You shouldn't swear like that son." he says. "If those wheels fall off again, just say, 'Praise the Lord!'"

Just then, the wheels do fall off again. "Praise the Lord!" says the boy. And the wheels just roll back to the wagon and attach themselves.

"_____!" says the clergyman.

Clue: You don't expect this from a priest. But it makes sense here. What did the boy say?

4) A rabbi gets caught in a rainstorm and ducks into a Chinese restaurant to wait it out. At the bartender's invitation, he takes a seat and accepts a complimentary Mai Tai.

Shortly, the rabbi, who usually does not drink alcohol, leans over and punches the bartender in the face. "That's for Pearl Harbor," says the rabbi.

"Pearl Harbor? Are you crazy? I'm Chinese, not Japanese."

Stories and Longer Jokes

"Ach, Japanese, Chinese. What's the difference? But I'm sorry if I offended you. Let me buy you a drink."

The bartender accepts, and a few minutes later, leans over and punches the rabbi in the face. "What was that for?" asks the startled rabbi.

"That's for the Titanic!"

"The Titanic? That was destroyed by an iceberg."

"Ah," says the bartender, shrugging his shoulders, "iceberg, _____, what's the difference?"

Clue: The clue is "iceberg." What's a common Jewish name? Remember, he wants to get even.

5) A local resident runs over Mrs. Tipson's cat. He knocks on her door and says, "I'm sorry Mrs. Tipson, but I'm afraid I've just run over your cat. But don't you worry, I'll replace him."

"Then don't just stand there. There's a _____ in the kitchen."

Clue: She took him literally. What would the cat do in the kitchen?

6) A woman is conducting a survey on sexual behavior, and she asks an airline pilot, "When was the last time you made love to a woman?"

He answers, "1956."

She is startled, and repeats, "1956?"

The pilot adds, "Well, it's only _____."

Clue: Find another way to interpret "1956."

7) The Godfather calls up an escort service and says: "I want a special girl. She has to be exactly 6 feet 6 inches tall, weigh less than 80 pounds, and have red hair."

They look at each other, puzzled, and he says, "Shut your face! Just do it! Bring her to me today, wearing a white sun dress."

PUNchline

All hell breaks loose as they search for this woman, but a call finally comes back: "Godfather, we found someone who has red hair and weighs only 78 pounds, but she's only 6 feet and 3 inches tall. But we could put her in 3-inch heels."

"Bring her to me within the hour," says the Godfather.

The woman arrives shortly, clad in a long white sun dress. The Godfather nods his approval, then goes into the next room, and returns with a little red-haired girl in a white sun dress.

He stoops down to the little girl and says: "See what grandpa tells you? If you don't _____ you'll _____."

Clue: He's using the woman to make a point. What do Italian mothers and grandmothers always (stereotypically) try to get their (grand) children to do?

8) A stranger walks into a bar, orders a drink, and then pulls out of his pocket a small toy piano. Then he pulls a mouse out of the other pocket. The mouse sits down at the piano, and starts playing the most amazing ragtime piano you ever heard.

The bartender is dumfounded. He says, "Hey, that's great!" Then the man takes a canary out of another pocket, and sets him on the piano. And the canary starts warbling all the songs the mouse is playing. The bartender is even more impressed. So he offers the man $5,000 for the act, and the man takes it.

On the way out, another man calls the stranger aside, and says, "You made a big mistake selling that act for $5,000. You could have gone all over the world and made hundreds of thousands of dollars."

And the stranger says, "Naw, I don't think so. People don't realize it, but that canary can't sing a note. The mouse is a _____."

Clue: This makes the act even more incredible than before. Who were Edgar Bergen and Charlie McCarthy?

Stories and Longer Jokes

9) My grandmother lived to be 99. One day, I asked her, "What's your secret?" and she said, "I just make myself get out of bed every morning." So I thought, "Well, that's not too tough, but how do you make yourself get up?"

And she said, "It's easy. I just _____ before I go to bed."

Clue: This is something that would really work, and makes sense even in a non-joking way. What could you do the night before that would leave you no choice but to get out of bed?

10) There was a woman who came in every day to see her doctor in a Health Maintenance Organization. There was nothing wrong with her, but everyone listened patiently, and actually looked forward to her visits. One day, she didn't show up. She even missed the day after that. When she came in the next day, everyone asked, "Where were you the last two days? We missed you."

She said, "To tell you the truth, _____."

Clue: It's just the opposite of the explanation you expect in this particular situation, although it fits what we generally say in circumstances like this.

11) A man is told by his doctor that he only has 12 hours to live, and when he gets home, his wife asks him, "What would you like to do?" And he says, "Make love." So they go into the bedroom and make passionate love.

A couple of hours later, they come out of the bedroom, and she asks him, "Well, you've got 10 hours left, what would you like to do?" And he says, "Make love." So they go at it again.

Then she asks, "Well, you've got 8 hours left, what would you like to do?" Once more, he says, "Make love." And she says, "That's easy for you to say, you _____ _____."

PUNchline

> *Clue:* A remark that suggests he's being inconsiderate, and that would be appropriate in any other context other than this one. It's a phrase we sometimes use when we're up late.

12) A man (give him the identity of anyone you want to put down) goes ice fishing. He cuts a hole in the ice, but then hears a loud voice say, "There are no fish there!"

    Although startled at this, he moves over to another location and begins cutting a new hole. Again, a voice booms, "There are no fish there!"

    He tries a new spot, and the voice repeats, "I said there are no fish there!"

    "Who is that?" he cries out. "Who's talking to me?"

    "The _____," says the voice.

    > *Clue:* It's not God. In this joke, you're trying to make the person look stupid. So think of a situation where there's ice, but where there couldn't possibly be fish below.

13) A speaker says to his audience, "We've all heard the phrase, 'Nobody's perfect.' If there's anyone here who's perfect, just raise your hand, because I'd really like to meet a perfect person."

    No one raises their hand at first. But then he notices a middle-aged man way in the back waving his hand back and forth. "Great!" says the speaker, "We've finally found a perfect person. Tell me sir, are you really perfect?"

    "No, no, no," said the man, "I'm raising my hand for_____."

    > *Clue:* It's someone else. But who? What bad habit do previously-married couples often have when annoyed with their new spouse?

Stories and Longer Jokes

14) An avid golfer hooks his ball into the woods, and goes searching for it. While looking, he comes across a leprechaun who is brewing a strange concoction in a small pot. "Whatever are you making?" asks the golfer, "It smells great!"

"It's a magic brew," says the leprechaun. "If you drink it you'll become such a good golfer that you'll never again be defeated."

"Well, let me have a drink of it then," says the golfer.

"As you wish," says the leprechaun, "but I must warn you that it has a serious side effect. It will sharply lower your sexual desire."

"I can live with that," says the golfer, taking half a dozen big gulps. And sure enough, the golfer never loses another game. Within six months, he's declared regional champion. He's so delighted with this that he goes back to the woods to thank the leprechaun. "It worked," he says, "I'm the best golfer anyone's ever seen around here."

"Yes, but how's your sex life?" asks the leprechaun.

"Pretty good," says the golfer, "I've had sex three or four times in the last six months."

"That doesn't sound very good to me," says the leprechaun.

"Well," says the golfer, "It's not that bad for a _____."

Clue: There's no trick here. Just think of someone who you don't expect to have sex very often — if at all.

15) The Episcopal church assigns a woman pastor to a small town parish. The women like her, but the men have their doubts. She likes to fish, so when the men get together a fishing party, she asks to go along.

The men are so distracted by her presence in the boat that they get to the middle of the lake, and discover they left the bait on the dock.

PUNchline

The pastor says, "Well, there's no sense in us all going back. Wait here." And she climbs out of the boat and walks across the water back to the dock.

One of the men says, "Isn't that typical? They send a woman pastor to a fishing town, and she can't _____."

Clue: A remark that would normally make sense, but completely overlooks the incredible feat of walking on water.

16) In the early-Gorbachev years, a firm sends a man to the USSR to close a deal. He's convinced they'll be spying on him. The Soviets put him in a fine hotel, but he knows it has to be bugged. He searches for hours, and finally finds it under the bed — a plate attached to the floor with a single nut. He quickly disassembles it and goes to sleep.

The next morning, the desk clerk asks if he noticed anything unusual or had any trouble during the night.

"No, not at all, why?"

"The people in the room under you did. Early this morning, _____."

Clue: What if the thing he disconnected wasn't a bug, but a functional part of the building?

17) The time has come for St. Peter's annual 3-week vacation, so Jesus volunteers to fill in for him at the Pearly Gates. "It's no big deal," explains St. Peter. "You just sit here at the registration desk, and ask each person a little about his or her life. Then send them up to housekeeping to pick up their wings."

In the second week, Jesus looks up to see a tired-looking old man in front of him. "I'm a simple carpenter," explains the old man. "But I once had a son. He was born in a very special way, and was unlike anyone else in the world. He went through a great transformation, even though he had holes in his hands and

Stories and Longer Jokes

feet. He was taken from me a long time ago, but his spirit lives on forever. People tell his story all over the world."

"Father!" Jesus cries out. "Its been so long!"

The old man squints, stares for a moment, and says, "_____?"

Clue: It wouldn't be a joke if it were really God. Who else fits the bill?

18) Lenny is selling Sal, a good buddy, a suit. "I'm telling you Sal, you get a quality suit like this, and even your best friend won't recognize you. Just take a walk outside a bit and get the feel of it."

Sal goes out, and returns a few minutes later. Lenny rushes up to him and says, "Good morning _____ _____?"

Clue: This is predictable (although absurd), given what Lenny has just said to Sal.

19) A well-known brain surgeon was taking reporters on a tour of the hospital's new brain transplant facility.

"These," said the doctor, "are secretaries' brains, at $3,000 a pound. And here are some salesmen's, brains, at $8,000 a pound. And these are executives' brains, at $40,000 a pound."

A puzzled reporter interrupted, "Wait, why are the brains of executives so much more?"

"Young man," said the doctor, "Do you realize _____?"

Clue: Look for some kind of reversal of the assumptions you're making here.

20) Back in the old west, an Irishman, an Italian, and a Chinese decide to become partners and start a mining operation. The Irishman runs the office, the Italian is made general foreman, and the Chinese is in charge of supplies.

PUNchline

The mine quickly becomes successful, but the Chinese is missing. Fearing foul play, the other two partners search the storehouse, and then the mine — nothing!

Finally, in the most remote part of the mine, just as they are about to give up in despair, the Chinese partner jumps out of the shadows with a big smile on his face, and shouts, "_____!"

Clue: Remember, he's Chinese. And what is he in charge of? And what peculiarities of sound occur when Chinese speak English?

21) One day a man was startled to find God talking to him: "I have big plans for you. Prepare!"

So he went out and got a facelift, a hair transplant, liposuction, contact lenses, and a new wardrobe. On the way home, he was run over by a bus, and found himself standing in front of the Throne. "If you had such big plans for me, Lord, why did you let me get hit by a bus?"

The Lord shrugged, "I didn't _____."

Clue: You need to reject the assumption that the Lord knows everything. Remember, he made a lot of changes in his appearance.

22) Back in 1985, the Pentagon had just developed a new computer that could understand and answer human voice commands. Suddenly, an alarm sounds, lights start flashing, and a synthetic computer voice says, "The Soviet Union has launched a nuclear attack."

One of the generals shouts to the machine: "Is the attack coming from land, sea, or air?"

"Yes," answers the computer.

"Yes, what?" screams the general.

"Yes, _____!" answers the computer.

Clue: What is always expected when addressing a superior officer?

Stories and Longer Jokes

23) It was early afternoon, and the boss — Mr. Condon — announced that he was going home early for the weekend. All of his employees were sure that he was going to play golf, and wouldn't be calling in, so they all left too after a while.

  But when Sam, the accountant, came home, he found Mr. Condon in bed with his wife. So he quietly slipped out and went to a movie.

  The next friday, Mr. Condon again announced that he was going home early. And all the employees again started leaving — except for Sam. "What's the matter, Sam?" someone asked. "You can leave. He won't be back."
  "I know," replied Sam, "but I left early last week, and almost _____."

  Clue: His reaction to what happened the week before reflects a concern which is just the opposite of what you'd expect. What should the boss be concerned about in this situation?

24) A well-known mafia figure being tried for murder bribes one of the jurors to hold out for manslaughter — forever, if necessary. The jury is out for 29 hours, and finally returns a verdict of manslaughter. After the trial, the defendant says to the bribed juror, "Listen, I appreciate that! Did you have any trouble?"
  "I'll say I did," he answers. "I had a really tough time of it. I held out for manslaughter, just like you asked. Everyone else wanted _____."

  Clue: It wouldn't be funny if the answer was "murder."

25) Some years ago, there was a congressman who went to an Indian Reservation to speak to a large group of Indians in his district.

  "My good friends, I shall see to it that the government helps you."

  "Oom Galla!" shouted the Indians.

  "I shall see to it that you have better schools."

PUNchline

"Oom Galla!" they shouted again.

"I will work for better housing for you, and jobs for those who want them."

"Oom Galla!"

"I will see to it that you get federal grants."

"Oom Galla! Oom Galla!"

After his speech, he was chatting with some of the Indians about their problems, when he suddenly noticed some very handsome prize bulls grazing in a meadow nearby. He said, "They're really spectacular animals. Do you mind if I walk over and have a closer look?"

"OK," said the chief, "But be careful you don't step in the _____."

Clue: You shouldn't need a clue for this one. An often-heard expression when you don't believe or trust someone.

26) In a public park, one night, a beautiful male statue and a lovely female statue were miraculously given life by a good fairy. After sitting motionless in the park for 35 years, they were alive! She looked at him, and he looked at her. And they knew what had to be. Hand in hand, the two former statues disappeared behind a large bush. Sounds of laughter and great joy came from behind the bush. Squeals of delight and pleasure were heard throughout the night. A passerby snuck a look behind the bush, and couldn't believe his eyes. The two former park statues were _____."

Clue: It's not what you think! It concerns pigeons. Remember, they used to be statues.

27) Quasimodo advertises for a man to ring the bells. The next day, a man comes in with no arms. "Are you kidding?" says Quasimodo.

"I'm serious," says the man. "I need the job. Just give me a chance."

"OK," says Quasimodo, "ring the bells. After all, who am I to discriminate against the handicapped?"

Stories and Longer Jokes

So the man runs up the stairs, takes a flying leap at one of the bells and rings it with his head — Boing! — and collapses in a heap. Then he picks himself up, takes a run at the second bell — boing! But as he runs at the third bell, he completely misses it, flies out the window, and falls to his death below.

A crowd gathers around the body, and when Quasimodo comes down, they ask him, "Who was this man?"

"Well, I never knew his name," he replies, but his face _____."

Clue: A familiar phrase for situations where we recognize someone, but can't remember their name.

28) The next day, another man with no arms applies for the bell-ringing job. Quasimodo says, "Amazing! I had a guy come in here yesterday that looked just like you."

"I know," says the man, "that was my brother."

"Listen," says Quasimodo, "this is dangerous work for a man with no arms. Look what happened yesterday."

But the man refuses to leave, so Quasimodo eventually gives in and lets him ring the bells. But exactly the same thing happens. The first two leaps at the bell are ok, but on the third, the man flies out the window and falls to his death."

Again, when Quasimodo comes down, they say, "Who was this man?"

"I never knew his name," says Quasimodo, "but he's a _____ for his brother."

Clue: Again, find a familiar phrase that fits the situation.

29) Back in the old west, two New Yorkers hear about the war between the settlers and the Caringee Indians. Since the Caringees were killing all settlers in sight to win back their lands, the government was offering a $1,000 bounty on the heads of all Caringees brought in — dead or alive. They decide to head out west in order to cash in.

PUNchline

During their first night on the range in Caringee territory, they fall asleep dreaming of the possibilities for riches. The next morning, one of them wakes up to discover that they are surrounded by hundreds of Caringees. He pokes his partner, and shouts, "Wake up! Wake up! We're _____!"
Clue: The punchline assumes they (think they) are in control of the situation.

30) An American psychiatrist was touring the UK and visited a home for the dangerously insane. There were many sad cases, but he noticed one man laying colored bricks in lovely mosaic patterns in the garden. "That's beautiful!" he said to the worker.
"Thanks, I built it all myself."
"Where's your studio?"
"I don't have a studio. I'm a patient here."
"A patient? Good heavens, man, you're an artist! When I get back to London, I'll call the director and have you paroled. I know many wealthy Londoners who'll commission you to design one of these for their garden. You'll be wealthy within a year."
"You'd do this for me?"
"Of course! Well, here's my bus. I'll be in touch."
Just as the psychiatrist is climbing into the bus, something hits him on the head, and he falls back down the steps. After a minute, he looks around to see what hit him. It's a colored brick. He looks over to his artist/patient friend, who smiles and says, "_____!"
Clue: Think of any remark that makes it clear that he really does belong in the institution.

31) Three businessmen are arrested in a Latin American country, and sentenced to death by firing squad. As they were taken out to be shot, the lawyer says, "They don't look very bright. Let's trick them."

Stories and Longer Jokes

The lawyer was chosen to be shot first. After "Ready . . . Aim . . ." he said, "Typhoon!" The firing squad ran for cover, and the lawyer escaped.

The banker tried a similar tactic. "Ready . . . Aim . . ." and he shouted, "Tidal wave!" Again, everyone ran for cover, and he escaped.

Then it was the salesman's turn. After "Ready . . . Aim . . ." he screamed, "_____!"

Clue: Think of a disastrous event which would normally distract people, and make the execution less important, but which would have the opposite of the intended effect here.

32) An 90-year-old man goes to confession and tells the priest: "I made love to 3 beautiful women last weekend."

"For your penance, you should say the Rosary," said the priest.

"What's that?" said the old timer. "I'm not Catholic."

"You're not Catholic? Then what are you telling me for?"

Said the old timer: "I'm telling _____!"

Clue: He's not there because he feels he's done something wrong. Remember, he's 90 years old.

33) A banker calls up an optimistic Texas oil man to review his loans. "We loaned you a million dollars to perk up your old wells, and they went dry."

"Coulda been worse," says the oil man.

"Then we loaned you a million to drill new wells, and they were all dry holes."

"Coulda been worse," replies the oil man.

"Then we loaned you another million to buy new equipment, and it all broke down."

PUNchline

"Coulda been worse," says the oil man.

"And I'm tired of hearing that!" snaps the banker. "How could it have been worse?"

And the oil man says, "It coulda been _____ money."

Clue: An answer that suggests that the oil man himself hasn't really been hurt by this at all.

34) An early believer in cryonics was thawed out 50 years later, and began to panic when he realized that he no longer qualified for any kind of job. Then he remembered his investments, and called up a broker to check their value. "Thirty million dollars," he was told.

He was beside himself with joy — until the operator said, "Your three minutes is up. Please deposit _____ _____."

Clue: Consider exaggerated inflation.

35) Goldstein, a salesman, spotted an Arab lying in the sand, while driving through the Negev desert. He rushed over, picked him up, and showed him an exquisite collection of ties. "Are you in luck! I have here the best selection of ties you ever saw."

The Arab whispered, "Water! Water!"

"Look, for you, a special bargain, five dollars."

"No, I need water . . . please!"

"Well, you drive a hard bargain. Four dollars is the best I can do."

"Pul-eeze, give me some water!"

"Oh, you want water? Well, no problem. You just head over that dune, and turn right and in about 1/4 mile, you'll find the Camel Club. They'll give you all the water you want."

So the Arab slowly crawled over the sand dune, and with his last ounce of strength, pulled himself up to the front door of the Camel Club. "Water!" he begged, "Give me some water."

Stories and Longer Jokes

"You want water?' You came to the right place. We got well water, seltzer water, whatever kind of water you want. The only thing is, you can't get in _____ _____."

Clue: Look for irony. Why was the salesman put in the story?

36) A couple in a large van was driving along when a rabbit suddenly darted across the road. There was no way to avoid it. Splat! They stop and go back to look at it. The husband says, "Well, there's nothing we can do to help him now."

"Yes there is," says the wife. She runs back to the van and comes back with a spray can. She sprays the dead bunny, and while they watch, the bunny comes back to his natural form. He gets up and hops across the road, pauses, waves good-by, hops some more, pauses, waves goodby, and finally hops into the woods.

"That's incredible!" says the husband, "What's in that can?"

She shows him the label, which reads, "_____ restorer with permanent _____."

Clue: A product someone might use if they were bald.

37) In a saloon in the old west, the door swings wide open, and in walks a dog — on its hind legs. He waddles up to the bar, and says, "Gimme a whiskey!"

The bartender is enraged, and orders the dog out. The dog refuses. So the bartender reaches down, grabs his six-shooter, and shoots the silver dollar right out of the dog's front foot. The dog howls and yips, and runs out the door.

The next day, the same dog walks in, this time with a six-gun on each hip. All talk stops as the dog looks slowly around the room and says, "I'm after the man who shot my _____."

Clue: A familiar phrase from westerns.

81

PUNchline

38) An insurance salesman tried everything to get a client to buy life insurance, but he wouldn't budge. Finally, in desperation, the salesman says, "Ok, I've met my match. You're not going to buy. I can accept that. But in consideration of all the time I've spent with you, would you please sign this testimonial letter for me?"

The client reads the letter out loud: "This is to confirm that I will not buy insurance from you regardless of how hard you try to convince me that I should, or how good your arguments are."

"What kind of testimonial letter is this?" says the puzzled client. "Even if I did sign the letter, who could you show it to without feeling like a fool?"

The salesman says, "I'll show it to your wife, _____."

Clue: Under what conditions would his wife be annoyed that he didn't buy life insurance?

39) O'Malley owns a store that's just been burglarized. He meets his friend Kelly on the street. "I'm sorry to hear about the robbery," says Kelly. "Did you lose much?"

"Some," replies O'Malley. "But it would have been much worse if the burglar had broken in the night before."

"Why?" asks his friend.

"Well, you see, the very day of the robbery, I _____."

Clue: It's something he did in the store. What do you often do in order to sell more goods?

40) A terminated employee requested an exit interview with the human resources director of the company.

"I understand you have an issue?"

"An issue of what? I probably didn't read it."

"I mean you wish to protest."

82

"Well, I'm concerned about the environment, whales, and racial equality, but that's on my own time."
"I was referring to your position here."
"You mean the way I'm sitting?"
"Are you being straight here?"
"My personal life is my own business."
"Just tell me, why did your boss fire you?"
"He wouldn't tell me. That's why I'm here. He just said he couldn't _____ to me."
Clue: This interchange demonstrates the problem.

41) An eccentric businessman offering a large contract invited all interested competitors to dinner at his estate. After dinner, he took them outside and showed them his swimming pool — filled with hungry alligators. "The contract," he said, "goes to anyone who dares swim the pool from one end to the other."

Out of nowhere, a man jumped in and frantically splashed his way across the pool. He pulled himself out on the far side just inches ahead of the snapping jaws.

"Now that's heroic!" cried the eccentric. "The contract is yours."

"Thank you very much," said the man. "Now show me the guy who _____!"
Clue: No one would risk their life just to get a contract.

42) An old man calls in his grandson for a chat. "Johnny, you're thirty years old, single, no babies. We're worried. What's the problem?"

Johnny shrugs, "I haven't met the right woman."

"Ah," says the old man, "And what are you looking for?"

Without speaking, Johnny taps his forehead, then rubs his thumb and fingers together, and finally makes two open-handed gestures over his chest.

83

PUNchline

The old man nods. "Yes, brains are very important," he says, tapping his head. "And money certainly helps." Then, imitating the two-handed gesture over his chest, he asks,

"But why must she have _____?"

Clue: The old man has misunderstood the third gesture. What might an old man think of when two hands are held up in this fashion? Think of a medical problem associated with aging.

43) Two friends were out hiking in the forest, when suddenly they came across an enormous black bear, seven feet tall! The bear was up on his hind legs, growling in anger.

One of the friends quickly lowered his pack to the ground, pulled out a pair of running shoes, and began lacing them on.

"Don't be ridiculous," said the other, "You can't outrun that bear!"

"I know," said the first, "but I don't have to outrun him, I just have to _____!"

Clue: Put the emphasis on "him," not on "outrun."

44) The star running back of the college football team was about to fail English, and flunk out of school. The coach called up the head of the English Department, and begged him to give the student one last chance.

"Ok," said the English professor, "Send him over."

So the student goes over, and the professor says, "I'll ask you just three questions. Get one of them right, and you pass. First question: How many days of the week begin with the letter 'T'?"

The student mulls it over, and says, "Two! Today and tomorrow."

"Let's move on to the next question. How many seconds are there in a year?"

84

Stories and Longer Jokes

Again, after considerable thought, the running back says, "Twelve! January 2, February 2 . . ."

"Let's skip right to the third question. Since Christmas is coming soon, tell me how many times the letter 'D' appears in the title of the song 'Rudolph the Red Nosed Reindeer'."

The player squinted and seemed to be running the song title over and over in his mind. Finally, he answered: "Seven!"

"Seven? How did you come up with seven?"

The athlete counted on his fingers as he hummed, "_____."

Clue: What sound do people use when they hum songs?

45) A prominent looking gentleman lost his wallet at a dance.

"Excuse me!" he announced, standing on a chair, "But I lost my wallet with $600 in it. I'll give $50 to anyone who finds it."

A voice from the rear shouted, "I'll give _____!"

Clue: No clue needed.

46) Sam and Tony owned a clothing store. When Sam returned from vacation, he was startled to walk in and find his partner walking on crutches, and bandaged from head to toe.

"My God, what happened?" he asked.

"You remember that purple and green checked suit with the narrow lapels that we've been stuck with for years? I sold it!"

"So what happened to you? The customer didn't like the suit?"

"The customer loved the suit," said Tony, "but his _____ nearly killed me!"

Clue: Who would buy such a suit? He'd have to be blind.

PUNchline

47) Two salesmen had a run of hard luck, and got stuck in a small town in Montana with virtually no money. They heard that the hills had a lot of wolves, and that wolf pelts sold for $40 a piece. So they rented a gun, and bought 6 shells and a knife with the last of their money, and set out for the hills.

They made a little fire, and fell asleep as the sun set. A little later one of them was startled out of his sleep by a long eerie howl. He looked out at the bushes around the dying fire and found that they were surrounded by hundreds of snarling wolves.

He shook his buddy, and said, "Wake up, we're _____!"

Clue: You've already seen this joke in another form. (Notice how easy it is to make different jokes from the same punchline.)

48) Carson's beer ran a nation-wide contest for a new slogan. The top prize was one million dollars. Thousands of entries came in, and a winner was finally selected. It stated: "Carson's beer: Like a cabin by the lake." It was the basis for a multi-million dollar ad campaign across the country.

Then Mr. Carson came by the ad agency and asked, "What does it mean? Why is Carson's beer like a cabin by the lake?"

There was immediate panic. No one had thought to ask. They set out to find the contest winner, and asked him, "What does it mean? How is Carson's beer like a cabin by the lake? Just tell us, and we'll double the prize."

"Because," he said, "It's about as close as you can get to _____."

Clue: This turns out to be a put-down of the beer. What's a common criticism of some "light" beers?

Stories and Longer Jokes

49) One day an elderly couple came to a sex therapist, and asked him to counsel them on their sexual technique. He did, and told them that everything was fine — that they really had no problems.

They paid his $25 fee, but came back again the following week, and the week after that. After the sixth demonstration, the doctor said, "You two are not only normal; you're very good sexual partners. Why do you keep coming back?"

The man said, "Well, Doc, this kind of thing ain't covered by Medicare, and at $25 a visit you're cheaper than _____."

Clue: They aren't married, and need a place to have sex.

50) A man has a fight with his wife, and goes to a bar to cool off. After two beers, he phones home to apologize.

"Hello, honey, it's me. What're you makin' for dinner?"

"What am I makin', you bum? Poison! That's what!"

"Well just make _____! I'm not comin' home."

Clue: How can he turn the tables on her?

51) A man walks into a bar with his dog. The bartender says, "Get out! We don't allow dogs in here."

"Wait a minute," says the man. "This is no ordinary dog. He can talk."

"Sure he can," says the bartender. "If he can talk I'll give you a hundred bucks."

The man puts the dog on a stool and says, "Ok Blackie, what do we call the top part of a house?"

"Roof!"

"Right. And what's on the outside of a tree?"

"Bark!"

"Good. Now let's try something a little tougher. Name a surrealist French sculptor."

PUNchline

"Arp!"

"Terrific! And who would you say is the greatest baseball player of all time?"

"Ruth!"

The bartender is furious. "Listen pal, get that dog out of here before I throw you both out."

As soon as they get out on the street, the dog says, "_____?"

Clue: What if the dog really could talk?

52) A small town barber was widely known for his know-it-all attitude and tendency to put people down. Yet almost everyone liked him. One client had this exchange with the barber:

"Going on vacation this year?"

"Yeah, to Rome."

"Lot of pollution and crime there. But you can always stand in St. Peter's Square and see the Pope."

"Yeah, I'm hoping to get an audience with him."

"You, an audience? The Pope sees Kings and Presidents. Why would he want to see a small-timer like you?"

"I just hoped I could see him privately."

"Well, forget it. You've got nothing he wants."

A month passes, and the guy is back for a haircut. The barber asks: "How was Rome?"

"Great! I saw the Pope!"

"From St. Peter's Square, of course, with the crowd."

"Yes. But then the darndest thing happened. Two guards pushed their way though the crowd to where I was standing, and one of them says, "The Pope would like to see you."

"So I went along with them, right into the Vatican, and up to the Pope's private apartment. And there he is, just waiting for me with this big smile on his face."

"You wanted to see me, Holy Father?"

Stories and Longer Jokes

"Yes, I did. I noticed you there in the crowd. Do you mind my asking you a personal question?"

"Of course not, Holy Father."

"Fine," says the Pope, "I just wanted to know, where did you get that _____?"

Clue: What's one way to get even with the barber for his constant put-downs? What might the Pope notice about the visitor from his balcony? What is the visitor's link with the barber?

53) A college student received a phone call from his brother Tom, back home. "Your cat's dead," said Tom.

The student fell apart and started crying uncontrollably.

"Damn it Tom," said the student, "couldn't you break it to me a little more gently? You could have said, 'Your cat got up on the roof, and we couldn't get it down'. Then you could say, 'It fell as it tried to jump to a tree'. And then you could tell me 'it died after the fall'."

"I'm sorry," said Tom. "You're right. I was crude."

A couple of weeks later, the student again got a call from Tom, who said, "Grandpa _____."

Clue: Their grandfather has just died.

54) A well known comedian died and woke up in the presence of a man in a white flowing robe. He wondered where he was.

The man said, "I have examined your life, and have decided that you deserve this." He presented the comic with 30 pages of the most beautifully written material he'd ever seen: The Golden Script! There must have been an hour and a half of hilarious material there, with each line funnier than what came before it.

The comic looked up with tears in his eyes: "So, I'm in Heaven, then?"

89

PUNchline

"Not exactly," smiled the other, "You've gone the other way."

"Then why have you rewarded me with this wonderful material?" asked the comic.

The man answered, "What are you going to do for _____?"

Clue: What would be real Hell for a comedian?

55) A famous acting teacher was telling her students about the worst actress she'd ever seen. She was so bad, no one would hire her. But then she married a rich producer who included her in all his shows. Once he produced a stage adaptation of *The Diary of Anne Frank*. Her portrayal of Anne was so bad that when the Gestapo came searching for her, the handful of people still in the audience stood up and shouted, "She's _____."

Clue: This is a different kind of humor. How can they get even with her for her bad acting?

56) A conductor on a passenger train was caught throwing people under the wheels of the train when he thought no one was looking. At his trial, he was found guilty of first degree murder, and sentenced to die in the electric chair. The judge told him he was a terrible representative of his profession.

On the execution day, he survived three massive jolts of electricity without any apparent injury. "How could this be?" asked the warden.

"Well, like the judge said," sneered the doomed man, I'm a _____."

Clue: Find a link between electricity and his profession.

57) A country church had a surplus of funds, and the financial committee asked the pastor for a recommendation on how to spend it. The pastor suggested a chandelier. The committee

Stories and Longer Jokes

thanked him, and began their deliberations. The pastor was later told the request had been denied. He asked why.

"Because," the chairman explained, "In the first place, none of us could spell it; in the second place, none of us could play it; and in the third place, what the church really needs is more _____."

Clue: It's precisely what the pastor requested.

58) Frank Perdue (who has his own brand of chicken products in supermarkets) visits the Pope, and says, "I'm willing to donate a million dollars to the Catholic Church in exchange for one word."

"What word?" asks the Pope.

"A word in the Lord's Prayer," says Frank. "Just change 'Give us this day our daily bread' to 'Give us this day our daily chicken'."

"No, I couldn't possibly do that," says the Pope. "Well, think about it," says Frank.

The next day, Perdue is back. "OK, I'll make it two million dollars if you make it chicken. Not bread. Chicken."

"No, it can't be done," says the Pope.

"Well, think about it," says Frank.

The next day, Frank is back again. "Well, these are my tickets to head back home today. This is your last chance. Five million dollars to your church in exchange for a single word: chicken! Not bread. Chicken!"

The Pope sighs deeply, and calls in his top Cardinal. "Yes?" asks the Cardinal. The Pope says, "How firm is our deal with _____?"

Clue: If the Pope had made a financial deal in connection with The Lord's Prayer and some other product, what product would it be?

91

PUNchline

59) A newlywed said to his bride: "Every time we make love, I'm gonna put a dollar bill in this metal box." And true to his word, as the months passed, he stuffed a dollar in the box every time they engaged in marital bliss. But the time came when he had to go on a lengthy business trip. He took his wife's picture, and every time he dreamed of making love to her, he mailed her a dollar.

When he arrived home, he said, "Darling, let's see how much we've saved." They opened up the box, and out fell a bunch of $5, $10, and $20 bills. "How is this possible?" he asked. "I only gave you one dollar at a time!"

"Yes, darling," said his wife, "but _____ _____!"

Clue: If money is put in the box only after she makes love, and he only gives her $1 bills, and he's been away on a trip . . .

60) On her death bed, a woman was expressing her final wishes to her husband of many years. "Dominick, you've been so good to me all these years. I know you never even thought about another woman. Now that I'm going, I want you to marry again as soon as possible, and I want you to give your new wife all my expensive clothes."

"I can't do that darling," he said. "You're a size 16 _____."

Clue: Her assumption about his fidelity is entirely wrong.

61) The patient cleared his throat in embarrassment before explaining his unusual problem. "YOU SEE DOC," he boomed in a voice so deep and raspy that it was hard to understand, "I CAN'T GO ON WITH THIS VOICE ANYMORE — IT'S DRIVING ME CRAZY! CAN YOU FIX IT SO I SOUND LIKE A NORMAL PERSON?"

Stories and Longer Jokes

"I'll certainly try," said the doctor. After examining the patient, he reported that some sort of weight was pulling down on the vocal cords, loudening and distorting the voice. "Any idea what it could be?"

The patient cleared his throat again. "ACTUALLY, DOC, I HAPPEN TO BE . . . UH . . . ESPECIALLY WELL-ENDOWED, AND MAYBE THAT'S WHAT'S DOING IT! BUT LISTEN, IF YOU HAVE TO REMOVE SOME OF IT, THAT'S OK WITH ME! I'LL DO ANYTHING TO GET A VOICE LIKE A REGULAR GUY!"

So the doctor went ahead with the operation. The patient telephoned two weeks later. "Hey doc," he babbled happily, "I can't thank you enough. I finally sound just like anyone else. I can lead a normal life — it's just great! By the way, doc, what'd you do with the piece of my penis you removed?"

"I _____."

Clue: The exact answer you give here is not as important as the way you say it.

62) Sylvia had lived a wonderful life, having been married four times. Now she waits at the Pearly Gates. St. Peter says to her: "I notice that you first married a banker, then an actor, then a priest, and finally an undertaker. What kind of system is that for the life of a good Christian woman?"

"A very good system," Sylvia replies.
"One for _____, two for _____, three to _____, and four to _____!"

Clue: Think of the childhood equivalent of "On your mark . . ."

63) A man with terrible financial woes stands on the edge of a bridge, poised to jump, when he hears a voice: "Go down to the Casino!"

93

PUNchline

He obeys the voice, and goes down to the Casino. When he gets in, he hears the voice again: "Roll the dice!" He does, and wins — again and again. Each time, the voice says, "Let it ride!" Finally, with over half a million dollars on the table, he realizes his financial troubles are over. As he reaches over to sweep it in, the voice again says, "Let it ride!" Slowly, and reluctantly, he moves it back, and promptly loses the whole pile.

"What now!?" he screams out.

"_____," says the voice.

Clue: You don't expect the voice that saved him to now give up on him, but . . .

64) Before the fall of the Berlin wall, a teacher in an East Berlin school room asks little Hans to give an example of a dependent clause.

"Our cat has a litter of 10 kittens," he answers, "all of which are good Communists."

"That's excellent," says the teacher. "You have a good grasp of grammar, as well as the Party Line."

Several weeks later, a Government Inspector visits the school and the teacher again calls on Hans.

"Our cat has a litter of 10 kittens," he repeats, "all of which are good Western Democrats."

"That is not what you said a few weeks ago," snapped the teacher with embarrassment.

"Yes," replied Hans, "but the kittens eyes _____ now."

Clue: Hans has learned some things about Communism he didn't know before. You also need to know a little about how kittens develop in the first few weeks of life to understand this joke.

65) A man who is petrified of flying makes his way to his seat, and gets a strangle hold on both arm rests. A stewardess sees this and decides to try to comfort him.

Stories and Longer Jokes

"You look nervous," she said, "Do you fly often?"

"No," he said, "I travel by train. It's safer."

"Well, I don't know about that," she said. I read in the paper just last week about a passenger train going through the desert with nothing around it for a hundred miles. Then, all of a sudden, it derailed and exploded. All the passengers were killed."

"My God!" said the passenger. "What happened?"

"A _____ fell on it," said the stewardess.

Clue: What's the one thing that might fall on the train that would do anything but calm the passenger's anxiety about flying?

66) A salesman traveling through Northern Ireland had to spend a night in a Belfast hotel. He was told he'd be safe as long as he stayed in his room between sundown and sunrise.

His room had no TV, and there wasn't much to do in the hotel. By 10 p.m., he had read the papers, and was having a nicotine fit. From his window, he could see a small shop at the corner which seemed to be open. He decided to risk it.

He crept down the stairs, out the back door, and just as he approached the shop, he ran smack into a hefty man with a stocking over his head, and a gun in his hands. The man asked: "Are you Catholic or Protestant?"

The salesman began to panic, but his thinking was clear. "If I say 'Protestant,' and he's I.R.A., it's over. If I say 'Catholic,' and he's Protestant, that's no better." So on an impulse, he says: "I'm _____."

The gunman looks up to Heaven, and says, "Allah be praised!"

Clue: No clue necessary.

Sometimes the improbable occurs.

PUNchline

67) A man looked up to Heaven and said, "Please, God, let me win the lottery. I've been a good man all my life. I've been a good husband and a good father. I've never hurt anyone in my life."

    He looked for his name in the paper the next day, but it wasn't there. This time he got down on his knees, and said, "God, why did you let me down? Please let me win the lottery. What do you have to lose?"

    A deep voice boomed down from the heavens: "Do us both a favor. Buy _____!"

Clue: What is the one absolute prerequisite for winning the lottery?

68) A diplomat in Rome was commonly known to drink too much at official functions. At the reception for a foreign dignitary, he had started drinking long before the affair began.

    As the formal evening began, the orchestra struck up a tune just as a vision in white swept by him toward the receiving line.

    With a gallant bow, he whispered: "Lovely creature, dressed in white, waltz with me this summer night."

    The other stopped, looked at him and said, "No, I won't dance with you, and I'll give you three good reasons why. First, you are intoxicated. Second, this is not a waltz; it's the Italian National Anthem. And third, I am _____."

Clue: Who is the most famous person in Rome?

69) There was a terrible brush fire in a field near the high school, and the principal called the volunteer fire department. Soon, the 40-year-old fire truck comes barreling by the gathering crowd, its sirens blowing and the bell ringing. It pulls off the main road, and without even slowing down, heads directly into the center of the burning field. Fifteen volunteers jump off the truck with shovels and sand and hoses, and they gain control of the fire within a mater of minutes.

Stories and Longer Jokes

The crowd applauds them loudly, and a local reporter walks over to the soot-blackened chief, and says, "Cap'n Donnelson, that was the bravest thing I ever saw. Protecting the high school by driving right into the center of the blaze, and not even considering your own safety. Could you say a few words for townspeople to read in tomorrow's paper?"

"Yes," said the chief, "Tell 'em to vote us the funds to _____ that damn truck!"

Clue: If they really hadn't planned on driving into the center of the blaze, what problem with the truck might have caused them to wind up there?

70) A good looking man walks into a bar in which four divorced women have gotten together for a drink. One of the ladies says: "Hi, I never saw you here before."

"No, it's my first time here."

"New in town?"

"Yes, I just got out of prison after 25 years."

"Prison? How did you wind up in prison?"

"Well, I got mad at my wife one night and killed her with a hammer. Then I dismembered her body with a chain saw and put her in a dumpster."

"Girls, he's _____!"

Clue: The woman's reaction is just the opposite of what you'd expect, given his past.

71) Two (name any group you want to victimize) who were recent converts to Christianity arrive together at the Pearly Gates.

"We're running a little late today," says St. Peter, so I'll ask each of you just one question. Tell me," he asks the first man, "why do we have Easter?"

"That's easy," he answers, "it's the day Jesus was born."

"I'm afraid not," says St. Peter, "I can't let you in."

Then he turns to the second man and asks, "Do you know why we have Easter?"

PUNchline

"Certainly, that's the day that Jesus divided the Red Sea."
"I'm sorry," says St. Peter, "that's not good enough."
Finally he turns to the last man and asks, "And you. Do you know why we have Easter?"
He hesitates, but says, "Easter is the day Jesus was reborn."
"Excellent. Please continue."
"He was in the grave for three days."
"Very good. And then?"
"Well, after three days he saw his ____, and that meant they would have _____ weeks of _____."
Clue: February.

72) Two French Canadians, Luc and Andre, hired a bush pilot to take them by seaplane out into the wilderness to go moose hunting. They flew in at sunrise, and were to be picked up at sunset. All went well on the way in, but when the pilot returned, he found Luc and Andre with two large moose.

"You'll have to leave one of those moose behind," said the pilot, "the plane wouldn't get off the ground."

"Mais, no!" said Luc, "Last year a pilot take us out een same plane weeth two moose."

"Hmm," said the pilot, "I'm the best there is, so if another pilot did it last year, I can do it now. Ok, load 'em up!"

So, they loaded both moose, all the gear, and Luc and Andre into the little plane. The plane roared across the lake, struggling to lift off. It barely cleared the trees at the far side of the lake, but then stopped climbing. The pilot found a little clearing, and crash landed. Andre looked around: no one was hurt. "Well, Luc, how'd we do?" he asked.

"Pretty good," said Luc, looking around to get his bearings. "We got _____ than last year."

Clue: Luc didn't really say they got out successfully last year. What absurd way of thinking would lead them to be happy with how far they got before crashing?

Stories and Longer Jokes

73) A prominent biogeneticist is conducting research on the similarities between primates and humans. After a decade of careful preparation, he is preparing for his most daring experiment: the mating of a human with a gorilla.

He selects the perfect young gorilla, and then advertises in the New York Times to find the perfect human partner: "Wanted: Single white male, age 25-30, with a Master's degree, non-smoker, loves animals, to impregnate a female gorilla. Stipend: $500"

He receives over a hundred responses, and asks all of them to complete a lengthy questionnaire. Finally, he finds one who is the perfect mate. He says to him, "The job is yours, are you free to start Monday?"

"Just a minute," says the selected man. "I have a few conditions of my own. First of all, there'll be no kissing on the lips. Second, if there are any offspring, they must be raised in my own faith. And finally, could we wait a couple of weeks until I have a chance to raise the _____?"

Clue: He really wants to do this, and he misinterpreted the word "stipend."

74) The American Bar Association held their convention in New York, and three attorneys were sightseeing at the World Trade Center. As they stepped out on the observation deck, they were greeted by a mild mannered man standing on the very edge of the railing. "Hi!" he shouted, are you all lawyers from the convention?"

"Yes," said one, "now get down from there before you fall."

"Oh, don't worry, you can't get hurt falling from here."

"Oh, is that so?"

"Yes, they've installed giant fans on the 120th floor. If you fall from here, it triggers the fans, and they blow you right back up, safe and sound."

"That's absurd."

"Watch!" said the man, falling back over the rail. They rushed over to the edge, getting there just in time to see him reach the 120th floor. And sure enough, there was a giant "SWOOSH!" and he was blown safely right back up to the roof.

"It's great fun." he said. "You should try it."

So the three lawyers climbed up on the edge, linked arms, and jumped. Down they fell to the 120th floor, and nothing happened! They zoomed past the 90th, 60th, 40th, 10th . . . and SPLAAATT!

Two cops sadly viewed the mess on the sidewalk. "More lawyers?" said the first. "Yes," said the other, shaking his fist up toward the sky. "That damned _____ hates them!"

Clue: Who is the one (fictional) person who could achieve the feat of being blown back up to the roof?

75) An Amish farmer in Pennsylvania was driving along in a buggy when he was hit by a car and permanently injured. He sued for damages, and was being questioned by an attorney representing the insurance company. "Is it true that right after the accident you told the state trooper that you never felt better in your life?" asked the attorney.

"I did," said the farmer.

"No further questions."

The mediator asked the farmer to explain the circumstances which led up to that statement.

"Well," said the farmer, "I was lying there in the road with my horse and dog when the trooper came up. He saw my horse writhing in pain, and went over and shot him. Then he saw how badly hurt my dog was, and he shot him. Then he walked over to me and said, 'How're you feeling?' I said, '_____.'"

Clue: No clue is necessary here.

Stories and Longer Jokes

76) Young Paddy O'Grady left Ireland and came to New York and made a fortune in the construction business. Then he went home and married a girl from the village he grew up in, and brought her back to New York to live in a 30th floor penthouse. "All I ask," said Paddy, is that you keep it like you kept your father's house back home."

"I will," she said. And later that day, she disappeared.

Paddy was very upset, and called in both the police and private investigators to look for her. Four days later, she walked through the front door. "Thank God!" he cried, "but where have you been?"

"Washing _____."

Clue: What job that she might have had at home would take days to do in her new home?

77) A tractor salesman is driving up to a farm, and is startled to see a farmer lifting a large pig up to the branch of an apple tree. He watches in amazement as the pig bites an apple off the tree, and then the farmer puts him down. The procedure is repeated with several pigs. Finally, the salesman can no longer restrain himself. "Excuse me," says the salesman, "but wouldn't it be easier to pick the apples yourself and let the pigs eat them off the ground?"

"Might be," says the farmer, "but what would be the advantage of that?"

"Well, for one thing," says the salesman, "it would save a lot of time."

"Could be," says the farmer, "but what's time to a _____?"

Clue: Remember, it's not what you expect.

78) "Do you know what day today is?" she asked her husband at breakfast.

"Of course I do!" he answered.

In fact, he had no idea, but felt that he should know.

101

PUNchline

He spent the entire day trying to figure it out. Was it her birthday? No. Their wedding anniversary? No.

Something about the children? No. The anniversary of their first date? The day he proposed? What could it possibly be?

He decided that he could take no chances, so he came home that night with flowers, champagne, and diamond ear rings.

"Well, did I remember today?" he asked with a smile?

"You certainly did." she replied. It's the happiest _____ I've ever had."

Clue: It wouldn't be a joke if it were a date that really did turn out to be significant.

79) During the early days of Glasnost, the KGB wanted some favorable publicity, so they conducted their own investigation of the attempt to assassinate the Pope in St. Peter's Square. They interviewed dozens of people, examined thousands of photos, and poured over hours of videotapes. Finally, they announced their findings: "The Pope _____ first."

Clue: Self-defense.

80) Back in the 1950s, a train was speeding across the countryside during a rainstorm. The engineer didn't know that the rains had caused a torrent of water to roar down from the hills and destroy the bridge they were rapidly approaching.

A woman driving by spotted the washed out railroad bridge. She knew she had to do something to stop the train which would soon be coming around the bend. She had no flash light, no lantern. She had nothing but a clothes pin. As the train approached in the distance, she rushed over to the tracks and held the clothes pin up above her head. The white clothes pin stood out sharply in the engine's brilliant light. The engineer spotted it, and immediately slammed on the breaks, coming to a screeching stop 30 feet from disaster.

Stories and Longer Jokes

So, the question is, how did the engineer realize what the woman was trying to tell her?

Well, everyone knows that a clothes pin in the air means, "_____ on the line."

Clue: Find the word linking what clothes pins are normally used for to what happened to the bridge.

81) A man looking for an apartment in New York was walking along the East River when he suddenly heard a man in the river crying for help. "Where do you live?" cried the would-be rescuer. The drowning man shouted his address and the "rescuer" rushed to his apartment to claim it.

"It's already rented." said the landlord.

"It can't be!" cried the other. "I just left the current occupant drowning in the East River. Who could have gotten here before me?"

"The guy who _____."

Clue: How did the occupant wind up in the river to begin with? How desperate do people get when they're trying to find an apartment?

82) In the 1980s, an American manufacturer was showing his farm equipment factory to a potential customer from Albania. At noon, the lunch whistle blows, and two thousand men and women stop work and leave the building.

"Your workers, they're all escaping!" cries the visitor.

"Don't worry, they'll be back," says the American. And sure enough, the whistle blows again at one o'clock, and everyone heads back to their jobs.

After completing the tour of the factory, the manufacturer asks his guest, "Well, which of our products do you think you'd like to order?"

"Forget the farm equipment," says the Albanian, "What's the price of _____?"

103

PUNchline

> *Clue:* What problem did Soviet-bloc countries often have with their workers?

83) A preacher was going on and on and on during his sermon, when a man suddenly got up and started to leave. "Where are you going?" asked the preacher.
    "To get a haircut," said the man.
    "Well why didn't you get a haircut before you came in here?"
    The man answered, "Because I _____ _____."
    Clue: It was a very long sermon.

84) A politician storms into his speech writer's office: "That speech you wrote for me was terrible! It was too long! The first half was fine, but the second half was so boring that most of the audience got up and walked out on me!"
    The speech writer says, "I gave you _____ that speech."
    Clue: In fact, the speech the politician gave was exactly twice as long as it should have been. What would explain the entire second half being boring?

85) During a big fire in Yellowstone National Park in the 1980s, a photographer was assigned to get photographs of the blaze. He arranged for a small plane at a local airport to take him up to get the photos. He arrived at the airport, and found a Cessna waiting near the gate with its motor running. He jumped in with all his equipment and shouted, "Ok, let's go!"
    The pilot took the plane out to the end of the runway, and they were up in a matter of minutes.
    "Fly over the park," said the photographer, "and make a few low level passes."
    "Why?" asked the pilot.

Stories and Longer Jokes

"Because I'm going to take pictures!" he snapped. "I'm a photographer, and photographers take pictures!"

After a few moments of silence, the pilot said, "You mean you're not _____?"

Clue: Neither person is who the other thinks he is.

86) An old recluse loved his cat so much that he tried to teach it to talk. "Then I won't have to bother with humans at all," he said.

He tried every technique he could think of to train it to talk. First he tried food he thought the cat would love, canned salmon and canaries. The cat was delighted, but never learned to talk. One day it occurred to him to feed his talkative parrot to the cat. He cooked the parrot in butter, and served it to the cat on a bed of catnip. The cat loved it. He licked the plate clean, and then — incredibly — suddenly turned to his master and shouted, "Look out!"

The recluse didn't move, and the chandelier came crashing down on his head, killing him instantly. The cat just shook his head and said, "He spends two years getting me to talk, and then the dummy doesn't _____."

Clue: No clue necessary.

87) Three lovely daughters approach their father to get his permission to marry. The father asks the first daughter: "Who do you want to marry?"

"He's in the Tater family," she answered. "He's an Idaho Tater."

"Why the Idaho Tater is a fine tater. I'd welcome him into our family."

"I want to marry a Tater too," said the second daughter. He's a Maine Tater."

"Another fine Tater." said the father. I'd welcome him as well. And who would you like to marry?" he asked the third daughter.

"Peter Jennings."

105

PUNchline

"Peter Jennings? Why he's nothing but a _____ tater!"

Clue: This is a pun. What kind of job does Peter Jennings have?

88) Two opposing sects of the First Century Christian Church struggle against each other for primary influence and power: the Essenes and the Herds. The Essenes believe that even children should qualify for church membership, while the Herds believe that membership should be restricted to adults. This may be the origin of the familiar view that "Children should be _____, but not _____."

Clue: Just play with the sound of the name of the two groups.

89) A chimpanzee walks into a bar, orders a whiskey, and puts $10 on the bar. The bartender gets his whiskey, and gives him his change — $2. And he says, "Pardon me for staring, but we don't get too many chimpanzees in here."

"Yeah," says the chimpanzee, "and at these _____ you won't see _____."

Clue: In this case, since the chimpanzee creates the strange circumstance, giving the normal response in this situation makes it funny.

90) A businessman who had been faithful to his wife throughout their 20-year marriage was in the midst of a mid-life crisis. While in another city on business, he spent an evening in a cocktail lounge, and met a woman. They spent several hours chatting over drinks, and one thing led to another — and they wound up in his hotel room.

The next morning, she asked: "I hate to ask you this, but just to put my mind at ease, tell me, is there any chance that you might have AIDS?"

"None at all," he said, "I've been faithful to my wife for 20 years. I'm not sure why last night happened, but there's no chance at all that I have AIDS."

"Thank goodness," she said, "I wouldn't want to catch THAT _____."

Clue: It's the man who ought to be worried here, not the woman.

91) The Magna Carta was touring the U.S., and a man known for his slow-wit went to see it on his lunch hour. The guide was explaining that it was the source of English freedom, and was signed by King John.

"When did he sign it?" the man asked.

"1215," said the guide.

"Damn!" said the man, looking at his watch.

"_____!"

Clue: Link together the signing date, the time of day, and the fact that the man's not too bright.

92) Frank was a man who believed in the profound meaning of numbers. He was born May 5, 1935, and was 55 years old. He had five children, and lived at 555 East 55th St. He had earned $55,000 for the past 5 years at Saks Fifth Ave.

On his 55th birthday, Frank went to the track and was amazed to find a horse named "Cinquo de Mayo" running in the fifth race. Five minutes before the race began, he went to the fifth window and bet $555 in five dollar bills on Cinquo de Mayo. And sure enough, the horse finished _____.

Clue: Would you really expect him to win?

93) An international law firm is advertising for a paralegal who can type, answer the phone, take dictation, and speak more than one foreign language.

They are startled to discover that the first applicant is a black and white Scottish terrier. They are even more amazed to find that the dog can type 120 words per minute, knows shorthand, and has an excellent telephone voice.

PUNchline

The personnel manager stammers, "You're really extraordinary, but what about the foreign language requirement?"

"_____," replies the dog.

Clue: From a dog's point of view, what might count as a foreign language?

94) A tremendous rainstorm is flooding a small town. A farmer on the edge of town is forced to crawl out of his house and on to the roof as the water keeps rising. As he sits on the roof, a neighbor comes by in a row boat and says, "Jump in, Hank."

"No thanks," says Hank, "I trust in the Lord. The Lord will save me."

An hour later, with the water still rising, the Coast Guard comes by and says, "You'd better come with us mister, they say the water's gonna keep on rising."

"No thank you. The Lord will take care of me."

Another hour later, it's still raining, and the man is forced to stand on top of the chimney, with the water lapping at his feet. Then a helicopter flies over, lowers a ladder down to him, and someone shouts, "This is your last chance! Grab the ladder and let us take you out of here!"

"No thanks! I trust in the Lord! I know the Lord will save me!"

Well, the man eventually drowns. When he gets to the Pearly Gates, he says to St. Peter, "How could this happen? I had complete faith that the Lord would provide."

From nowhere, a thundering voice booms, "Look, I _____."

Clue: Assume that the Lord does provide, but not always in the way we may expect.

95) In the 1970s, there was a Russian worker who wanted to buy a washing machine. There weren't any at the GUM (state store), so he asked the store clerk how he could manage to get one.

"Go to the factory and buy one," said the clerk.

Stories and Longer Jokes

"That's where I work! They won't even talk to me."

"Then do what everyone else does," said the clerk. "Just steal the parts, take them home, and build it yourself."

"I've done that twice," said the worker, "but each time it turned out to be a _____."

Clue: What did the Soviet Union pour most of its money into prior to Glasnost?

96) A man was cruising along in his convertible on a warm, sunny day on a country road, when he suddenly noticed a chicken running along side. But this was no ordinary chicken. It had 6 legs, and was running 40 MPH.

He accelerated, but the chicken kept up, running 50 MPH. He gunned it again. 60 MPH, and the chicken was dead even with him. He pushed it to 70 MPH. The chicken was still there, but was straining to keep up. Finally, at 80 mph, the chicken tired, and fell behind.

The driver stopped for gas in the next town, and described what happened: "I saw the damnest thing a few miles back — a 6-legged chicken running 70 MPH!"

"Oh," said the man, "it was probably from the Col. Sanders Experimental Chicken Farm."

"Of course!" said the driver, "a chicken with 6 drum sticks. Brilliant! They must be making a fortune."

"Not really," said the local, "I understand they haven't _____ yet."

Clue: If they're that fast, what problem might that pose?

97) Sister Lucretia lives in a very strict convent where the nuns have taken a vow of silence. They can speak only two words every 10 years. After 10 years, she goes to the Mother Superior: "Bed hard," she says.

Ten years later, she again meets with the Mother Superior: "Food bad," she says.

PUNchline

Still another 10 years go by, and it's time for another meeting with the Mother Superior. This time, she's so unhappy that she blurts out, "I quit!"

"It doesn't surprise me," comes the reply. "You've been coming here for 30 years, and _____."

Clue: What has she done at every opportunity?

98) Two very nervous young men got to talking in the doctor's waiting room and discovered they had similar symptoms. One had a red ring around the base of his penis, and the other one a green ring. The guy with the red ring was examined first, and came out all smiles in a few minutes. "Don't worry, man, it's nothing!" he announced cheerfully.

Greatly relieved, the second patient went into the examining room, only to have the doctor tell him a few minutes later, "I'm very sorry, but you have an advanced case of V.D. Your penis will have to be amputated."

Turning white as a sheet, the patient gasped, "But the first guy . . . he said it was no big deal!"

"Well, you know," the doctor pointed out, "there's a big difference between _____ and gangrene."

Clue: What sexual act could leave a red ring where this one occurred?

99) A woman went to a sex therapist, saying she was finding it increasingly difficult to find a man who could satisfy her, and that she was getting tired of short-term relationships. "Isn't there some way to judge the size of a man's equipment from the outside?" she asked.

"The only foolproof way is by the size of his feet," the doctor informed her.

So the woman went out and cruised the bars until she came across a man with the biggest feet she'd ever seen. She wined him and dined him, and took him back to her apartment, excited in anticipation of a night of sexual ecstasy.

Stories and Longer Jokes

When the guy woke up the next morning, the woman had already gone out. On the bedside table was $50 and a note that read, "With my compliments, take this money and go out and buy a pair of shoes that _____."

Clue: This still assumes that the doctor was right, so if this man disappointed her . . .

100) Miss Kline was grotesquely overweight, so her doctor finally prescribed a strict regimen, telling her it was the only way to avoid serious health problems in the future. "I want you to eat normally for two days, but then skip a day, drinking only water. Repeat this three times, and by the time I see you next Thursday you'll have lost at least 6 pounds."

The patient promised to obey, and showed up for the next appointment almost 20 pounds lighter. "Excellent progress," enthused the doctor, quite amazed. "And you lost all this weight by simply following my instructions?"

Miss Kline nodded. "But it wasn't easy doctor. On that third day, I thought I was going to die!"

"From hunger, eh?" said the doctor sympathetically.

"No, no," she explained, "from _____."

Clue: Look back at the doctor's instructions for the third day. She misinterpreted them.

111

ANSWERS TO STORIES AND LONGER JOKES

1) "Looking after my dog for a couple of hours?"
2) "Father time and mother nature."
3) "I'll be damned!"
4) "Goldberg."
5) "Mouse." ("Bowl of milk" would also work here.)
6) "2218 now."
7) "Eat your spaghetti, you'll look just like that."
8) Ventriloquist.
9) "Have a big glass of water."
10) "I was sick."
11) "You don't have to get up in the morning."
12) "Rink manager."
13) "My wife's first husband."
14) "A Catholic priest from a small parish."
15) "Even swim."
16) "Their ceiling light crashed to the floor."
17) "Pinocchio?"
18) "Stranger, what can I do for you?" (Or any other line which indicates that Lenny has not recognized Sal.)
19) "How many executives it takes to make a pound of brains?"
20) "Supplies!"

PUNchline

21) "Recognize you."
22) "Sir!"
23) "Got caught."
24) "An acquittal."
25) "Oom Galla."
26) "Relieving themselves on as many pigeons as they could find."
27) "Rang a bell."
28) "Dead ringer."
29) "Rich."
30) "Don't forget!"
31) "Fire!"
32) "Everybody."
33) "My."
34) "80 thousand dollars for the next three minutes."
35) "Without a tie."
36) "Hair . . . wave."
37) "Paw."
38) "After you die."
39) "Marked everything down 20%."
40) "Talk."
41) "Pushed me!"
42) "Arthritis?"
43) "Outrun you!"
44) "De-de de de-de de-de . . ."
45) "$100!"

Stories and Longer Jokes

46) "Seeing-eye dog."
47) "Rich!"
48) "To water."
49) "A motel."
50) "One portion!"
51) "Do you think I should have said DiMaggio?"
52) "Lousy haircut?"
53) "Got up on the roof."
54) "An audience?"
55) "In the attic."
56) "Lousy conductor."
57) "Light."
58) "Pepperidge Farms (or any other baker of bread)?"
59) "Other men aren't as stingy as you!"
60) "And she's only a 10."
61) "I THREW IT AWAY (note the significance of this being in capital letters)."
62) "The money . . . the show . . . get ready . . . go!"
63) "Go back to the bridge."
64) "Are open."
65) "Plane."
66) "Jewish."
67) "A ticket!"
68) "The Pope."
69) "Fix the brakes on."

PUNchline

70) "Single!"
71) "Shadow . . . six more . . . winter."
72) "Further."
73) "$500?"
74) "Superman."
75) "I never felt better in my life."
76) "The steps."
77) "Pig?"
78) "Ground Hog's Day."
79) "Fired."
80) "Wash out."
81) "Pushed him in."
82) "One of those whistles?"
83) "I didn't need one then."
84) "Two copies of."
85) "The instructor?"
86) "Listen."
87) "Common."
88) "Seen (Essene) . . . heard (Herd)."
89) "Prices . . . many more."
90) "Again."
91) "It's 12:30. I just missed it!" (Or any other remark which indicates that he interpreted 1215 to refer to the time of day.)
92) Fifth.
93) "Meow."

Stories and Longer Jokes

94) "Sent two boats and a helicopter for you."
95) "Tank (or any other kind of weapon)."
96) "Caught one."
97) "All you've done is bitch, bitch, bitch."
98) "Lipstick."
99) "Fit."
100) "Skipping."

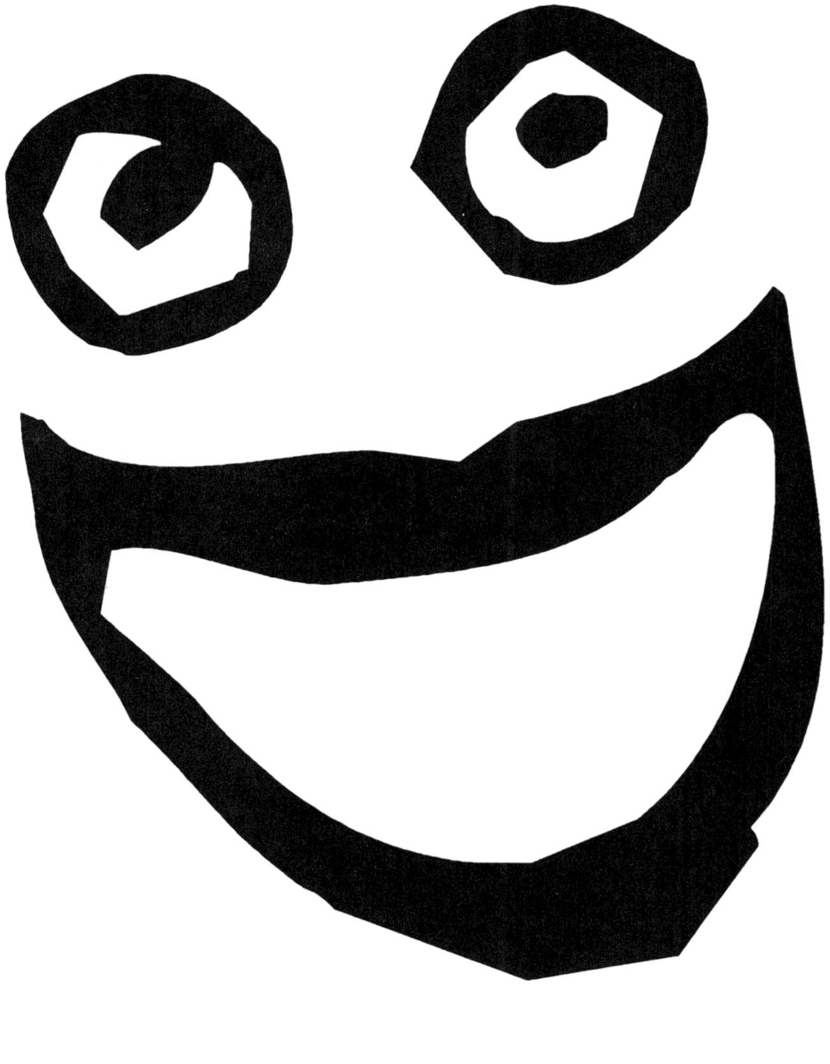

ORDER FORM
(for LAUGHTER REMEDY Products)

Payment may be made in the form of a check or money order, and must be received before shipping.

Name _____

Address _____

City _____ State _____ Zip _____

Item #   Quantity   Title   Unit Price   Total

_____

_____

_____

_____

_____

Shipping & Handling:
$10 or less $2.00
$10.25 to $20.00 ..... $3.00
$20.25 to $30.00 ..... $4.00
$30.25 to $40.00 ..... $5.00
$40.25 to $50.00 ..... $6.00

Subtotal _____
Shipping & Handling _____
New Subtotal _____
Sales Tax: NJ residents add 6% _____
Amount Enclosed _____

Mail to: **THE LAUGHTER REMEDY**
380 Claremont Ave., Suite 8
Montclair, NJ 07042
(201-783-8383)

ORDER FORM
(for LAUGHTER REMEDY Products)

Payment may be made in the form of a check or money order, and must be received before shipping.

Name _____

Address _____

City _____ State _____ Zip _____

Item #	Quantity	Title	Unit Price	Total

Shipping & Handling:
$10 or less $2.00
$10.25 to $20.00 ..... $3.00
$20.25 to $30.00 ..... $4.00
$30.25 to $40.00 ..... $5.00
$40.25 to $50.00 ..... $6.00

Subtotal _____
Shipping & Handling _____
New Subtotal _____
Sales Tax: NJ residents add 6% _____
Amount Enclosed _____

Mail to: **THE LAUGHTER REMEDY**
380 Claremont Ave., Suite 8
Montclair, NJ 07042
(201-783-8383)